WEEKEND
Rock

OREGON

WEEKEND Rock

trad and sport
routes from 5.0
to 5.10a

OREGON

RON HORTON

THE MOUNTAINEERS BOOKS

THE MOUNTAINEERS BOOKS
is the nonprofit publishing arm of The Mountaineers Club, an organization
founded in 1906 and dedicated to the exploration, preservation, and
enjoyment of outdoor and wilderness areas.

1001 SW Klickitat Way, Suite 201, Seattle, WA 98134

Manufactured in the United States of America

Acquiring Editor: Christine Hosler
Project Editor: Mary Metz
Copy Editor: Julie Van Pelt
Cover and Book Design: The Mountaineers Books
Layout: Jennifer Shontz, Red Shoe Design
Cartographer: Pease Press Cartography
Photo Overlays: Brian Metz
Photographs on pages 2, 5, 6, 28, 37, 42, 44, 51, 60, 78, 84, 88, 101, 107 (right), 134, 144, 148, 149, 156, 167, 170, 224, 228, and 236 by the author.
Photographs on pages 10, 14, 22, 66, 74, 75, 92, 105, 107 (left), 109, 121, 172, 177, 179, 180, 185, 202, 209, 212, 214, 216, 219, and 221 by Lynn Willis.

Cover photograph: *Maureen Pandos reads* Revelations *(5.9), Testament Slab, Christian Brothers Wall, Smith Rock.*
Frontispiece: *Michelle New reaches the anchors on* Edges and Ledges *at Broughton's Bluff*
Page 5: *Matt Bedrin preparing for the crux moves on* Scene of the Crime *at Bulo Point.*
Page 6: *Chris Smith on the entry moves of Flagstone's* Hydrotube.

Library of Congress Cataloging-in-Publication Data

Horton, Ron (Ronald Everett)
  Weekend rock Oregon : trad and sport routes from 5.0 to 5.10a / by Ron Horton.— 1st ed.
      p.   cm.
  Includes index.
  "Devoted to beginner and intermediate climbers."
  ISBN-13: 978-0-89886-717-6
  ISBN-10: 0-89886-717-7
  1. Rock climbing—Oregon—Guidebooks. I. Title.
  GV199.42.O7H67 2006
  796.52'209795—dc22

                                                                    2006019243

♻ Printed on recycled paper

Contents

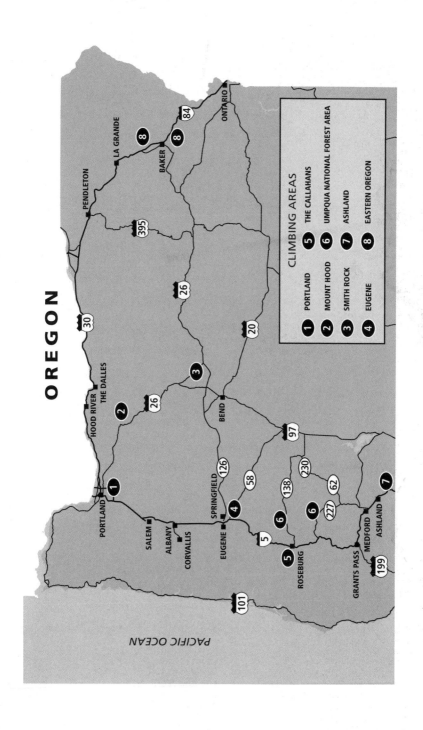

DESTINATION CHART

Destination	Drive time from Portland	Drive time from Bend	Drive time from Eugene	Drive time from Pendleton
PORTLAND				
Broughton's	20 mins	3–3¼ hrs	2 hrs	4 hrs
Carver	20 mins	3–3¼ hrs	2 hrs	4 hrs
Rocky Butte	10 mins	3–3¼ hrs	2 hrs	4 hrs
MOUNT HOOD				
Frenches Dome	1–1¼ hrs	2–2½ hrs	2½–3 hrs	3½–4 hrs
Salmon River Slab	1¼ hrs	2–2½ hrs	2½–3 hrs	3½–4 hrs
Bulo Point	1½–2 hrs	2–2½ hrs	3–3½ hrs	3½–4 hrs
SMITH ROCK				
Smith Rock	2½–3 hrs	35 mins	2½–3 hrs	4–4½ hrs
EUGENE				
Skinner Butte	1¾–2 hrs	2½–3 hrs	10 mins	5½ hrs
Flagstone	3–3¼ hrs	2–½ hrs	1–1½ hrs	6–6½ hrs
THE CALLAHANS				
Callahans	3½ hrs	4–4½ hrs	1¾ hrs	6½–7 hrs
UMPQUA NATIONAL FOREST AREA				
Honeycombs	3½–4 hrs	3½–4 hrs	2 hrs	6½–7 hrs
Acker	4½–5 hrs	4 hrs	3 hrs	7½–8 hrs
ASHLAND				
Emigrant Lake	5–6 hrs	4½–5 hrs	3½ hrs	8–8½ hrs
Greensprings	5–6 hrs	4½–5 hrs	3½ hrs	8–8½ hrs
Pilot	5–6 hrs	4½–5 hrs	3½ hrs	8–8½ hrs
EASTERN OREGON				
High Valley	4½–5 hrs	5½–6 hrs	6½–7 hrs	1½ hrs
Burnt River	5–5½ hrs	5½–6 hrs	7–7½ hrs	2–2½ hrs

Approach	Season	Rock Type	Climb Type
10–20 mins	Late Spring to Fall	Basalt	Trad/Mixed/Sport/TR.Cracks, Dihedrals, Face, Slab, Vertical
10–20 mins	Late Spring to Fall	Basalt	Trad/Mixed/Sport. Cracks, Face, Slab, Vertical
5–15 mins	Late Spring to Fall	Basalt	Trad/Mixed/Sport/TR. Cracks, Dihedrals, Face, Slab, Vertical
5 mins	Late Spring to Fall	Andesite	Sport. Face, Slab, Vertical
0 mins	Late Spring to Fall	Andesite	Sport. Face, Crack, Slab, Vertical
10 mins	Late Spring to Fall	Andesite	Sport/Trad/Mixed/TR. Face, Crack, Arêtes, Slab, Vertical, Overhangs
15 min–1 hr	Year Round	Welded–Tuff	Sport/Trad/Mixed/TR. Face, Crack, Arêtes, Dihedrals, Huecos, Slab, Vertical, Overhangs
0 min	Late Spring to Fall	Basalt	Trad/TR. Slab, Vertical, Overhang, Face, Crack, Arêtes
5–15 mins	Late Spring to Early Fall	Andesite	Sport. Slab, Vertical, Overhangs, Face, Huecos, Arêtes
10 mins–1 hr	Year Round	Sandstone	Sport. Slab, Vertical, Overhangs, Face, Huecos, Arêtes, Cracks
15–25 mins	Aug–Dec	Volcanic	Sport/Mixed. Face, Cracks, Slab, Vertical
½ hr–1 ½ hrs	Late Spring to Fall	Dacite	Sport/Mixed. Face, Slab, Vertical, Multi–Pitch
15–25 mins	Late Spring to Fall	Sandstone	Sport/Trad/TR. Face, Cracks, Arêtes, Dihedrals, Slab, Vertical, Overhangs
15–25 mins	Late Spring to Fall	Basalt	4th Class Scramble
20–35 mins	Early Fall to Late Spring	Andesite	Sport/Trad/Mixed/TR. Face, Cracks, Arêtes, Dihedrals, Slab, Vertical, Overhangs
5–15 mins	Early Fall to Late Spring	Basalt	Sport/Trad/TR. Face, Cracks, Arêtes, Slab, Vertical, Overhangs
5–25 mins	Early Fall to Late Spring	Limestone	Sport. Face, Broken Cracks, Slab, Vertical

Acknowledgments

I would especially like to thank several individuals for their help in turning the vision behind this book into a reality. Lynn Willis—friend, climbing partner, and photographer—put an immense amount of time into field research, shooting quality images, and scanning them for publishing. Maureen Pandos was always willing to travel and climb, and she was the original artist behind all of the route topos for this guidebook. My parents, Ron and Sandy Horton, provided an immense amount of support, both physical and mental, and I thank them for their guidance and encouragement throughout this writing process. Without the significant help of these people, I could never have completed this guidebook.

I would also like to thank the following people for their help with research, fieldwork, route climbing, and editing of this guidebook: Dana Griffin, Gary Smith, Jeff Walker, Brenden Thwing, Justin Couch, Matt Bedrin, Chris Call, Tim Dougherty, Evan Unti, Mike Newby, Chip Miller, Nat Crosman, Scott Shuey, Robert McGown, Sean Pierce, Eric Johnson, Jamie Flanagan, Jamie Brock, Ryan "Bird" Choate, Ryan Goldade, Jeff Bayha, Off White, Dave and Viviane Blythe, Hunter Lipscomb, Keri Taff, Kevin Pogue, Sandy Epeldi, Christopher Smith, Charles Schmidt, D. J. Herlehy, Radek and Shirley Chalupa, Chris McBride, Matt Stevens, Richard Humphrey, Kay Kucera, Stanley Pratnicki, Quinn and Willie, Christmas Rooster, Cody, Ruby, Truck, Eva Thomson, Christine Hosler, Maria Carantit, Mary Metz, and Julie Van Pelt. I would also like to express my gratitude to Matt O'Meara for introducing me to rock climbing, a sport that has changed my life.

Opposite: *View from Smith Rock's approach trail of the Crooked River with the Picnic Lunch Wall as a backdrop*

Preface

Over the past few years, climbing has soared in popularity, with a multitude of newcomers to the sport. This popularity has been spurred in part by the advent of indoor climbing gyms and artificial walls. Many people learn to climb on plastic, honing their skills to a high level, before ever even venturing outdoors or to the mountains. This year-round accessibility mixed with the dedication of athletes in search of higher limits has raised the bar for difficulty ratings around the world. Rock faces that were deemed unclimbable a quarter century ago serve as warm-up routes for today's top climbers.

This guidebook is not for those climbers. *Weekend Rock: Oregon* is devoted to beginner and intermediate climbers alike. It focuses on a wide array of climbs in a multitude of areas around the state. While it is by no means a comprehensive guide to climbing in Oregon, it does provide enough detail and description to help climbers navigate a path through some of the state's most beautiful areas as they climb both classic and lesser-known moderate routes along the way.

Routes included in this book range from challenging fourth-class scrambles to moderate traditional and sport lines. Traditional climbs range from 5.4 routes, where neophytes can learn to place gear, to intermediate 5.9+ test pieces such as *Gandalf's Grip* and *Moonshine Dihedral*. Sport climbs include 5.5 slab lines with bolts every 4 feet to 5.10b/c vertical and overhung face lines with a first bolt 15 feet off the deck. Routes rated 5.11 mark the beginning of advanced climbing, and 5.10d climbs are closer to these advanced ratings. Despite the subtitle, the cutoff for sport climbs in this guidebook is 5.10 b/c, which constitutes solid, intermediate 5.10 climbing. With the state's variety and diversity, *Weekend Rock: Oregon* includes a little something for everyone to enjoy.

Prior to *Weekend Rock: Oregon*, climbers wanting information about these areas needed to seek a wide range of publications to gather details. Most areas included in these pages have been published previously in a variety of small, local guides as well as in larger regional guidebooks. Portland climbing areas are covered in detail, and Frenches Dome and Bulo Point (in this book's Mount Hood chapter) are briefly described in Tim Olson's *Portland Rock Climbs*. Smith Rock is covered in detail by Alan Watt's *Climber's Guide to Smith Rock*, with updates by Ryan Lawson and the

Smithrock.com website. Southwestern climbing areas, including Ashland, Eugene, and the Umpqua Valley, are highlighted in Greg Orton's series of three regional guidebooks covering the Rogue, Umpqua, and Willamette valleys. Eastern Oregon is not covered in any major guidebook, and although websites and local guides do exist, they are hard to come by, as privacy is highly regarded in that area.

Having purchased these guides, beginning and intermediate climbers would then have to sort through several thousand climbs, most well beyond their climbing ability. *Weekend Rock: Oregon* provides a hearty sampling of highly enjoyable, if not classic, climbs from each destination included. Routes are chosen for their ratings as well as their quality, the result being a collection of some of Oregon's finest rock climbing that should occupy climbers for many weekends to come. I sincerely hope that you have as much fun exploring these routes as I did in the research and creation of this guidebook.

Introduction

Welcome to *Weekend Rock: Oregon*, the latest addition to the Mountaineer's Weekend Rock Series. This guidebook is intended for use by beginner to intermediate climbers who wish to visit multiple destinations in Oregon for recreational climbing on moderate routes. While it does include close to twenty different areas across the state, it is not an exhaustive nor definitive guide of every route in those areas. Each chapter is treated as a destination to visit over a weekend, a week, or several weekends. The number of climbs for each area ranges between twenty to thirty, with roughly twice that amount for Smith Rock, as it is Oregon's premier climbing area with well over a thousand established routes. This book can be used in unison with other guides to get a better overall view of all routes, or it can be used as a stand-alone guide to classic moderates around the state.

Many other climbing areas around Oregon are not included in this book for several reasons. Some have a majority of advanced routes, well beyond the 5.10a cutoff for this series (not that some liberties haven't been taken with that upper limit). Other areas were left out because they lacked classic moderates or because moderate climbs were too spread out over a wide area. Still other areas were left out due to current or potential future access issues. No one wants to write or publish a guidebook that leads to the closure of a cherished, local area. For example, Madrone Wall in Portland was omitted because it has been closed for years, although future access is still under debate.

While some individuals look down on having their area included in a guidebook, others embrace the necessity of sharing information, explaining access issues, addressing safety concerns, and listing rules for the usage of these unique climbing destinations. Eastern Oregon in particular has been long considered an untapped gem of rock climbing, with little to no information published on this immense section of the state. While much of the climbing in this region is sparsely located, there are several areas with moderate climbs, although many lie in backcountry regions of the forest and see little traffic. This guidebook is designed to provide the recreational climber with a series of diverse destinations to visit and explore while climbing classic, moderate routes.

Opposite: *Climbers at Smith Rock's Zebra Area on the Morning Glory Wall*

OREGON ROCK CLIMBING

The history of Oregon rock climbing is rooted in the history of mountaineering. Early pioneers and newcomers to the area were fascinated with the multitude of peaks the state had to offer and began systematically aspiring to reach the summit of each one. In many ways, bouldering and rock climbing were seen as mere practice for the more serious endeavor of climbing mountains. This concept began to change shortly after World War II, when Oregon climbers began to summit some of the smaller peaks at Smith Rock, the Wallowas, the Blue Mountains, and other areas in the state. Aid climbing was the main style used by these early pioneers until the mid-1960s. This form of rock climbing involves using natural pro or fixed gear not only to protect falls but also as handholds or aid in attaining the summit.

Free climbing, which is the sole focus of this guidebook, does not use any extra gear to help the climber reach the summit; all moves are completed by the climber alone with no extra aid. This form of climbing uses natural pro or fixed bolts to protect a climber's potential fall only, not for support. When a person first climbs a route, it is categorized as either a first ascent (FA) or a first free ascent (FFA.) The first person to climb a new route on a rope gets the FA, but the FFA goes to the person that has lead the route from the ground up, placing protection along the way.

Free climbing began gaining popularity in Oregon in the mid-1960s, and it continues to be the main focus for most local rock climbers. Next to bouldering and free-soloing rock faces without the use of even ropes for protection, free climbing is the purest way to reach the top of a climb.

Once free climbing gained a foothold in the Pacific Northwest, early climbing pioneers all over Oregon began establishing routes still considered intermediate to advanced by today's standards. Smith Rock, the Umpqua Valley, Portland, Ashland, Eugene, and other areas around the state began to see traditional free-climbing route development throughout the 1960s, '70s, and '80s. Many of these routes are included in this guide and still see regular traffic from local climbers as well as from visitors from around the world.

In the mid-1980s, the new style of free climbing known as sport climbing began to take hold in Oregon, and Smith Rock was one of the main areas responsible for this shift in styles. Since routes up most of the large rock outcroppings had already been established, local route developers began rappeling in from the top of the cliffs, setting up shorter routes on the lower walls that had remained unclimbed. Employing these methods—deemed radical for the time—created a schism in the free-climbing world between traditionalists and sport climbers, similar to the more modern rift between skiers and snowboarders. Although most climbers have overcome their initial suspicion of the new sport and embraced bolted climbs along with their earlier traditional forms, some die-hard individuals still deem sport climbing inferior in concept and practice to traditional climbing—much as the early mountaineers considered the sport of rock climbing frivolous compared to the art of mountaineering. While this guidebook focuses on rock climbing rather than mountaineering, it gives no preference to one form over another, putting traditional, mixed, and sport climbs alongside one another.

Each section of this book contains a brief history of the individual area, giving credit to that region's pioneers and early route developers. Oregon still has an abundance of unclimbed and/or unpublicized climbing areas, and many established areas still have an abundance of new route potential for future generations to come. Most areas also have a tight-knit group of local climbers still establishing quality lines, both traditional and sport, although some wish to keep their playgrounds less publicized than others.

ACCESS ISSUES

Since the mid-1990s or so, climbing access issues have become an ever-increasing problem. With the sport gaining popularity each year, there are simply more people visiting these climbing areas. This increased traffic makes for greater environmental impact, thus leading to more regulations imposed by land managers. While there are several local climbing coalitions within Oregon, the Access Fund (*www.accessfund.org*) remains the strongest nationwide group advocating solutions to the ever-growing problem of land use and its effects on climbers.

Access to climbing areas is an issue that varies in different regions of the state and during different seasons. There is no clear set of rules that applies to the state as a whole, so pay close attention to special rules in the introduction and beta box of each chapter. The overall rules that apply fall into four different categories: private land, state park land, national forest land, and Bureau of Land Management (BLM) land. When traveling to the various destinations in this book, climbers need to respect private-owner, state park, Forest Service, and BLM rules alike, in order to preserve the access and beauty of these areas for future visitors as well as for the local inhabitants.

While each chapter lists specific access issues for the climbing areas included within, there are some general overall rules that apply to all areas: stay on posted trails, avoid crossing land boundaries with No Trespassing signs, pack out what you pack in, obey all seasonal closures such as raptor nesting or fire, and be sure to adhere to all parking or land-use fees posted at designated spots.

For privately owned land, each area has its own set of rules. For instance, the owners of Carver Bridge Cliffs in Portland require visitors to become members of the Carver Climbing Club by paying a one-time fee and carrying photo ID while they climb. Greensprings, a privately owned area outside of Ashland has no established set of rules or fees to climb, but users of this area still need to be aware that they are on someone else's land. Use common sense and respect when climbing on private property. Obey all general rules listed in the paragraph above, and be sure to pay attention to any specific rules listed in the beta box for each area.

For the other three categories of land ownership—state parks, national forest, and BLM—all rules apply for the type of land in question. For state parks, see *www.oregonstateparks.org/searchpark.php*; for national forests, see *www.fs.fed.us/r6/r6nf.htm*; and for the BLM, see *www.blm.gov/nhp/info/index.htm*. A few of this guide's climbing areas are located in city parks, and regulations for these areas are discussed in that area's beta box.

Most every trailhead in Oregon's national forests requires a trail park pass, which can be purchased in most outdoor stores as well as at ranger stations. Many BLM areas require day-use fees, but some are free-use areas. Fees at state parks vary; some are free, while others require a day pass or parking pass. Yearly passes for all state parks can also be purchased at most outdoor stores as well. Paying day-use fees and camping fees enables land managers to maintain these beautiful areas, which is another way of promoting future access to Oregon's various climbing destinations.

Seasonal closures also affect the state's climbing areas. The two main types of closures for Oregon are due to fire danger and raptor nesting, specifically the peregrine falcon. While raptor nesting closures are similar from year to year, closures due to fire danger or burns fluctuate yearly and are generally dependent on weather. These closures do not generally affect climbing in Portland, the Mount Hood area, or in Eugene, but they do affect the rest of the areas in this book. For southern Oregon, the best resource for checking seasonal closures is a website maintained by Greg Orton, at *www.climbsworegon.com*. The state parks, national forest, and BLM websites listed above will also give you updated information about closures. Obeying these seasonal closures is crucial to maintaining future access to these climbing areas.

WEATHER AND CLOTHING

Oregon is a large and very diverse state. Weather can be drastically different in one region than it is in another on any given day. Altitude, climate, topography, and weather patterns differ from region to region as well. Weather can even differ from one destination to another within the same chapter of this book. For instance, the Mount Hood chapter describes Frenches Dome and Salmon River Slab, which are to the west of the mountain, and Bulo Point, which is to the east, bordering the desert. It can be raining on the west-side crags while it is still dry and warm on the east-side cliffs that face the desert.

Each area lists the best season to climb. In general, the farther northwest the destination, such as Portland and Eugene, the earlier the rain will begin in the fall. Roseburg and Ashland tend to stay dry longer, but not all winter. Higher-altitude areas, such as Frenches Dome, Salmon River Slab, Bulo Point (all in the Mount Hood chapter), Pilot Rock, Greensprings (both in the Ashland chapter), Flagstone (Eugene chapter), the Honeycombs, and Acker Rock (both in the Umpqua chapter), close when snow makes the Forest Service roads unnavigable. These closures are dependent on weather and seasonal snowpack. Smith Rock hosts year-round climbing, although the summers are brutally hot and the winters are intensely cold. This heat is magnified in eastern Oregon, and the climbing season there is generally in the fall and spring. Check each area's beta box for the best time to climb and specific details about that region.

Weather is a shaky science at best, and despite forecasts conditions can change quickly, especially in the mountains. The best rule of thumb is to visit a weather website, and check out the forecast for the closest city to your climbing destination. For clothing considerations, prepare for extremes. While the weather can be blistering hot in the daytime at many areas, even in the fall and winter, temperatures can change drastically after the sun goes down. Always pay attention to weather reports, know the general temperature trends for the season, and be prepared with extra clothing for all occasions.

GEAR CONSIDERATIONS

It is important to bring the proper gear to each area to ensure safety and enjoyment of that region. While you could belay from your car in some areas, the majority require a hike to reach the crag, and some approaches are more difficult than others. Each chapter lists climbing gear you should bring, but there are ten essentials that should be included in your pack for each area that requires a hike. These items should also be kept in your car any time you venture off the beaten path in case the unexpected occurs and you become stranded.

TEN ESSENTIALS: A SYSTEMS APPROACH

1. Navigation (map and compass)
2. Sun protection (sunglasses and sunscreen)
3. Insulation (extra clothing)
4. Illumination (headlamp or flashlight)
5. First-aid supplies
6. Fire (fire starter and matches/lighter)
7. Repair kit and tools (including knife)
8. Nutrition (extra food)
9. Hydration (extra water)
10. Emergency shelter

EXTRA GEAR

While the above ten essentials are important for hiking and backcountry trips, there are several other important items to bring on a climbing trip. One of the most important is an extra belay/rappel device. Another essential for many of the areas in this book is extra locking carabiners or quicklinks for lowering off of bolted anchors that only have webbing and no fixed rappel rings. It is also smart to bring extra webbing, because some of these areas are climbed less frequently than others, and the webbing at anchor/belay stations can be brittle or worn. It is not a bad idea to bring an extra rope to some areas too, for double-rope rappels or in case your rope gets stuck. Another item that can come in handy is an adjustable wrench to tighten loose bolts or anchors in some of the more remote climbing areas. While these items may not be considered essential, being prepared for the unexpected is the best way to avoid potential epics and ensure enjoyment for everyone involved.

STANDARD GEAR

The standard gear necessary to free climb the areas in this guidebook is as follows: set of 15–20 quickdraws in varied lengths, webbing of various lengths to create anchors or replace old rappel stations, extra locking carabiners, and a 60-meter rope (two 60-meter ropes for some rappels).

A traditional free-climbing rack for Oregon contains at least one set of wired nuts with doubles in some midrange sizes, a full set of three-cam units (TCUs) to ½ inch, and a full set of four-cam units from ½ to 4 inches with doubles in midrange sizes.

A NOTE ABOUT ANCHORS

Most anchors on the routes described in this guide are chain anchors, cold-shuts, or bolted anchors. Chain anchors and cold-shuts have links that you can feed rope through and lower off of without leaving gear. Bolted anchors, on the other hand, require the use of runners or webbing with quicklinks, which you leave behind.

EMERGENCY MEASURES

Each chapter gives phone numbers and street addresses of the closest medical facilities. Also listed is the location of the nearest pay phone. While many people have cell phones in this day and age, not all phones receive service in some of the remote areas listed in this book. It is a good idea to check the location of these phones before you venture off the beaten path into the noncellular backcountry to ensure that they are still in working order and that you know their exact location. A good portion of avoiding an epic in the outdoors entails being prepared for the unlikely event of an emergency and knowing your surroundings well enough to react quickly.

In case of an emergency, dial 911. In some remote areas, it may be important to stabilize the victim while someone goes for help. It is highly recommended to know basic CPR, if not wilderness first aid, when you choose to venture into the backcountry. If you have medical skills, stabilize the victim and send someone for help. In some densely wooded areas, it may be important to have the GPS coordinates to make locating the victim easier for rescue crews. In all emergency situations, do not

Chris Call balances up a featured arête at the Honeycombs.

react too hastily and become a victim yourself. Maintain a clear head, dial emergency services at 911, describe the victim's injuries and the location, and be prepared to assist rescuers in any manner necessary.

HOW TO USE THIS BOOK

This guidebook contains a wide variety of climbing areas across Oregon. Weather, clothing, gear, rock type, access, and local considerations all differ from area to area. Since the areas included are so diverse, each chapter has its own set of rules and information at the beginning to address issues specific to each destination. Each chapter has an introduction that details local history, early climbers, rock type, and other pertinent details. Each chapter also has a "beta box" that gives at-a-glance regional information, including general driving directions, climbing season, rules, camping areas, food and other amenities, emergency information, pet and child considerations, and other local activities.

The beta box is followed by a chapter's climbing areas, where you will find specific driving and trail approach directions as well as route descriptions. Where necessary, descent information is given at the end of a route description. Unless otherwise indicated, the descent is a rappel (for trad routes) or your choice of lower or rappel (for top-rope and sport routes).

RATINGS

The difficulty of a climb is set by the initial route setter and then agreed upon by subsequent climbers. Some ratings will differ due to a person's style and ability. A vertical to overhung sport climb rated 5.9 may feel completely different than a traditional crack climb or mixed slab climb of the same rating. Be certain to assess routes before you choose to climb, and stay within your comfort zone when choosing to lead new routes. The nature of the sport is that change is inevitable. Rock can crumble, holds can change, and fixed gear, bolt hangers, and anchors may be missing. Just over the course of writing this guide, I have witnessed missing bolt hangers, loose anchors, and crucial holds broken. Be prepared for the unexpected.

The climbs in this book range from fourth-class hikes such as Pilot Rock to fifth-class free climbs ranging from 5.0 to 5.10b/c. While these ratings work as a rough guide to the difficulty of a climb, they can vary between areas. Sport climb ratings and traditional climb ratings differ greatly as well due to the different types of climbing: crack, face, slab, vertical, and so on. Each area description notes whether the ratings are particularly stiff (harder climbing than the rating says) or soft (easier than the rating says). Some climb ratings have been adjusted from previous guidebooks if they are actually harder or easier than the original publication noted. These changes have been made through a consensus of local climbers or by first ascensionists who have decided that the climb's rating should be changed.

DIFFICULTY RATINGS

The climbs in this book are rated using the Yosemite Decimal System, which is the standard means of rating rock climbs within the United States. This system is broken down into five different classes, with the fifth class broken down further into decimals. The majority of this book falls into the fifth-class category, although there are some fourth-class climbs and several third- and fourth-class access trails.

The main fourth-class climb in this guide is the *Mountaineer's Route* on Pilot Rock (Ashland chapter), but some climber's trails at various areas would definitely be good examples of this grade as well. Many of the short descent trails at Rocky Butte (Portland chapter), the top-rope trails at Broughton's Bluff (Portland chapter), the Honeycombs (Umpqua chapter), and Greensprings (Ashland chapter), and the longer climbers access trail at Acker Rock (Ashland chapter) all qualify as fourth-class scrambles with potential rockfall and slide hazards.

Class 1: Walking on level ground with no obstacles.

Class 2: Trail walking or hiking with minimal obstacles: rocks, roots, holes, etc.

Class 3: Steep trails, scrambling, some use of hands, no need for ropes or gear.

Class 4: Steep to vertical scrambling, some obstacles need to be negotiated, could use ropes, potential consequences from fall.

Class 5: This is the beginning of technical rock climbing. Most climbers will want to use ropes and specialized gear to ascend. Class 5 climbing is further divided by decimals into 5.0 to 5.15. With the vision of a new generation of climbers and the advent of new gear, this decimal rating is growing.

Climbs from 5.7 to 5.9 may be given a + or - rating to further define difficulty. Starting at 5.10, climbs are often appended with an a/b/c/d, to differentiate difficulty even further. A 5.10a is more akin to a 5.9+, while a 5.10d is more like a 5.11-. The cutoff for this guidebook is 5.10b/c for sport climbs and 5.9+ for traditional climbs.

5.0–5.6: These climbs offer challenges for beginner climbers and are the standard entry level to technical rock climbing. Climbs may feature low-grade slab, highly featured face, or positive crack systems with solid placements.

5.7–5.9: These climbs become more challenging. This is a solid intermediate traditional leader category, but acts more as entry level for current sport climbers. Slab climbs become more vertical, face climbs have more sparsely placed holds and require more technical skills, and crack climbs may have less positive placements with thinner seams.

5.10–5.11: This category is generally considered intermediate. Climbing at this level requires dedication, practice, and even some specialized training. Again, traditional ratings and sport ratings differ, so be certain to know your limits before you attempt to lead any route.

5.12 and above: This level is considered advanced to expert. Climbs of this level are not included in this book.

The fifth-class climbs included in this guide vary between top-rope, traditional, mixed, and sport routes. Top-rope (TR) routes consist of climbs that have anchors that can be accessed from the top of the cliff or via a trail to a ledge. Top-rope problems are safest for beginners, because no one has to lead-climb the route to establish an anchor point for the rope. Rocky Butte (Portland chapter), Smith Rock, Skinner Butte (Eugene chapter), and Emigrant Lake (Ashland chapter), as well as many other areas covered in this book, all have top-rope areas for beginners and intermediates to practice their moves before leading other routes in the area.

QUALITY RATINGS

The quality rating in this book uses one to three stars. Each area stands alone in terms of its quality ratings, although no route has been given three stars unless it represents a classic by Oregon standards. A three-star climb at Smith Rock may differ drastically from a three-star route at Acker Rock due to rock quality, routefinding, anchors, and a variety of other factors.

Some longer climbs need to be assessed pitch by pitch. Just because one pitch of a climb receives a high rating does not mean that the entire route will be equally as good. Some second pitches of climbs are not included in this guidebook because they do not live up to the first pitch of the route.

Different rock quality and a climber's personal style and preference must be taken into account when assessing quality ratings on climbs. Most routes are in agreement with previous guidebooks, although some have been adjusted to fit the three-star system.

no stars: These routes are okay, but would not be a first choice to climb at the area.

★: Good climb, well worth including in this book. Some portions of rock may be lower quality, but the route is worth climbing.

★★: Excellent climb, a must-do for the area. Quality holds throughout.

★★★: A classic route, local test piece for the rating. These climbs contain fun moves throughout and represent the best in the area.

A NOTE ABOUT SAFETY

Safety is an important concern in all outdoor activities. No guidebook can alert you to every hazard or anticipate the limitations of every reader. Therefore, the descriptions of roads, trails, routes, and natural features in this book are not representations that a particular place or excursion will be safe for your party. When you follow any of the routes described in this book, you assume responsibility for your own safety. Under normal conditions, such excursions require the usual attention to traffic, road and trail conditions, weather, terrain, the capabilities of your party, and other factors. Because many of the lands in this book are subject to development and/or change of ownership, conditions may have changed since this book was written that make your use of some of these routes unwise. Always check for current conditions, obey posted private property signs, and avoid confrontations with property owners or managers. Keeping informed on current conditions and exercising common sense are the keys to a safe, enjoyable outing.

The Mountaineers Books

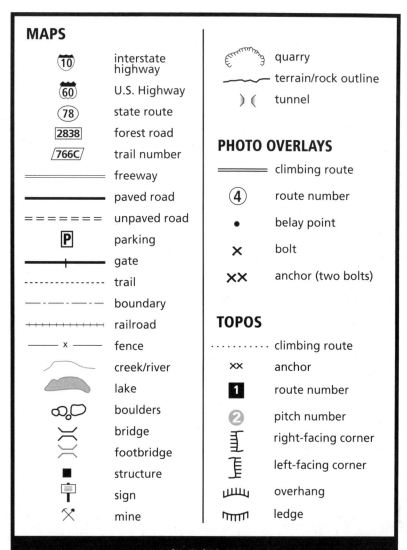

MAPS

(10)	interstate highway
(60)	U.S. Highway
(78)	state route
[2838]	forest road
/766C/	trail number
========	freeway
————	paved road
= = = = = = =	unpaved road
[P]	parking
——+——	gate
--------------	trail
—·—·—·—	boundary
+++++++++++	railroad
——— x ———	fence
	creek/river
	lake
	boulders
	bridge
	footbridge
■	structure
	sign
✗	mine

	quarry
————	terrain/rock outline
) (	tunnel

PHOTO OVERLAYS

========	climbing route
(4)	route number
•	belay point
✗	bolt
✗✗	anchor (two bolts)

TOPOS

············	climbing route
✗✗	anchor
1	route number
❷	pitch number
	right-facing corner
	left-facing corner
	overhang
	ledge

LEGEND

Portland

There are four main climbing areas in and around the Portland area. Unfortunately one of the finest, Madrone Wall, has been closed for nearly a decade. Broughton's Bluff, Carver Bridge Cliffs, and Rocky Butte still provide a wide variety of climbs on basalt rock ranging from cracks and dihedrals to slab, vertical, and overhanging face climbs. A weekend trip to Portland will provide climbers with a multitude of challenging routes within a 10- to 25-minute drive from the state's major metropolitan center.

Climbing development began at Broughton's Bluff in the early 1950s, with free climbing beginning in the late '60s. One of the first classic free routes, *Gandalf's Grip,* was established by Steve Strauch and John Hack in 1968 on the North Face, which is the main wall visible from the interstate and parking lot. The North Face is the farthest cliff left; all other areas are to the right of it on the side overlooking Crown Point Highway and the Sandy River. This area, consisting of ten major walls, has a wide array of climbs, both traditional and sport, ranging in difficulty from 5.5 to 5.13. This smooth basalt consists of cracks, dihedrals, column formations, and an abundance of featured faces on slab, vertical, and overhung rock. Many of the routes are mixed, with bolts placed on faces that yield no gear placements. The majority of routes must be

Mary Culbertson reaches for a high handhold while top-roping Ace.

led to be climbed, with the exception of some Red Wall and Hanging Gardens Wall routes.

Carver Bridge Cliffs was developed in the late '80s by local climbers Robert McGown, Jeff Alzner, Mark Simpson, and Tim Olson (the author of *Portland Rock Climbs*). There are three main walls and several smaller areas at this cliff, and they provide a variety of different climbing styles. The routes here range from cracks to featured face climbing between 5.4 and 5.13. Almost all routes must be led, as access to the top of the cliff is difficult, and many climbs do not top out. Aside from roped climbing, Carver has the best established bouldering in the greater Portland area. Carver Bridge Cliffs is located on private property, so you must become a club member and adhere to the rules (see Portland Area Beta). Be sure to obey trail closures in order to respect the owner and maintain future access, and always respect No Trespassing signs.

PORTLAND AREA BETA

Drive from Seattle	▲	3 hours
Drive from Eugene	▲	2 hours
Drive from Bend	▲	3–3¼ hours
Drive from Pendleton	▲	4 hours
Approach times	▲	5–20 minutes

Getting there: Broughton's Bluff is in Troutdale, just to the northeast of Portland; Carver Bridge Cliffs is near the town of Carver, southeast of Portland; and Rocky Butte is in Portland proper, east of downtown. See the individual areas for driving and trail approach directions.

Time to go: Portland weather fluctuates seasonally, so the ideal season is from late spring to early fall. You can climb year-round, but the access is sporadic due to rain. The Weather Channel's website is a good way to check weather (*www.weather.com*, search "Portland, Oregon"), or check with the National Weather Service at *www.weather.gov* or (503) 261-9246.

The rules: Broughton's Bluff is located in Lewis and Clark State Park, and Rocky Butte is a Portland city park. All state and local park rules apply to these areas. Visit *www.oregon.gov/OPRD/PARKS* or *www.parks. ci.portland.or.us* for more information on these two parks. Carver Bridge Cliffs is located on private property owned by the Rosenbaum family, and you must be a member of the Carver Climbing Club or you will jeopardize access. Sign a liability waiver and pay a one-time fee to join the Carver Climbing Club at the Portland Rock Gym, 21 NE 12th Avenue, (503) 232-8310, or visit *www.portlandrockgym.com* (as of May 2006, the fee is $8

---

cash or check only). There is a sign at the base of the Rockgarden Wall that gives contact information for a representative of the Rosenbaum family. Call (503) 224-3113 for more information. Carry photo ID at all times while climbing at Carver.

Camping: Closest to Broughton's Bluff is Ainsworth State Park (pets allowed). Closest to Carver Bridge Cliffs is Milo McIver State Park (pets allowed). Visit the Oregon Parks and Recreation Department website above for more information. For Rocky Butte, there is no park camping in the Portland metropolitan area, but both Ainsworth and Milo McIver State Parks are not far. The Portland International Hostel is in southeast Portland at 3031 SE Hawthorne Street, (503) 236-3380.

Food: For Broughton's Bluff, exits 16 and 17 off I-84 both have general fast food and grocery stores. For Carver Bridge Cliffs, the town of Carver has several dining establishments, and there are grocery stores and other amenities along OR 224. For Rocky Butte, the greater Portland metropolitan area has every type of food imaginable.

Climbing type: Cracks, columns, and face climbs on slab, vertical, and overhanging rock faces. Trad, mixed, and sport routes. Broughton's Bluff and Rocky Butte have top roping, but all Carver climbs must be led.

Rock type: Basalt

Gear: 15–20 quickdraws of varied lengths, extra locking carabiners, trad rack to 4 inches with doubles of midsize gear, webbing and runners of various lengths, 60-meter rope (2 ropes for some rappels). Some top anchors are missing at Rocky Butte, so bring a wide variety of webbing (recommended 30 feet or more in a variety of different lengths to equalize anchors as trees, bolts, and natural pro placements allow). A daisy chain is also recommended at Rocky Butte, as some anchors are below the cliffband and minimal downclimbing is required.

Emergency services: Dial 911.

Nearest hospitals: *Broughton's Bluff:* Legacy Mount Hood, 24800 SE Stark Street, Gresham, (503) 674-1122. *Carver Bridge Cliffs:* Kaiser Sunnyside Hospital, 10180 Sunnyside Road, Clackamas, (503) 652-2880. *Rocky Butte:* Providence Portland, 4805 NE Glisan Street, Portland, (503) 215-1111.

Pay phones: *Broughton's Bluff:* Glenn Otto Community Park. Pass Lewis and Clark State Park, continuing on Crown Point Highway roughly 0.25 mile to a stop sign. Turn right, crossing the river. Park is on the left at 1106 E Historic Columbia River Highway. There are two pay phones, one by the road and one in the park. *Carver Bridge Cliffs:* Convenience store at intersection of OR 224 and Carver Bridge Road. *Rocky Butte:* The intersection of 82nd and Fremont has several gas stations with pay phones.

Extras: Dogs are allowed at all spots, but they must be kept on a leash in state and city parks. The close proximity of the Sandy River to Broughton's Bluff and the Clackamas River to Carver Bridge Cliffs makes both areas ideal for dogs even in the heat of summer. Both are kid-friendly as well, but watch out for loose rock and steep cliffs at both places. The main cliffs of Rocky Butte are neither dog- nor kid-friendly, as the descent to the base of the cliff is either a fourth-class trail/downclimb or a rappel. The top of the cliffband is narrow and steep in spots as well. The top of Rocky Butte Road does have a city park overlook with a stone retaining wall for bouldering, and it is both kid- and dog-friendly. Aside from Olson's guidebook, visit the following sites for more information on Broughton's Bluff, Carver Cliffs, and Rocky Butte: Portland Rock Gym, *www.portlandrockgym.com*; Oregon Alpine Club, *http://ors.alpineclub .org/AAC/rocky1.html*; and the Carver bouldering page, *http://home .earthlink.net/~mrmrsabbott/Carver_Bouldering/Carver.html*.

Other local activities: Cycling, hiking, windsurfing, paddling, fishing, bouldering, disc golfing, and swimming.

Rocky Butte is the closest climbing area to downtown Portland. It saw major route development from the mid-1970s to the late '80s by climbers such as Robert McGown, Tim Olson, Mike Pajunas, Mike Smelsar, and Scott Woolums. It is the epitome of an urban crag. If this cliff were located anywhere else, it would qualify as some of the best basalt climbing in Oregon, but unfortunately it lies just above the intersection of two major interstates. Although belaying from the bottom works better for communication with your partner, the top of the cliff is within 5–15 feet of Rocky Butte Road, which leads to one of the city's most popular overlooks, so anyone passing by can access your anchors. Climbing web bulletins tell horror stories of stolen gear, anchors that have been tampered with, and unknown persons throwing rocks or bottles. Whether these are urban myths or not, the ideal scenario for climbing at Rocky Butte is to have a group climbing at the bottom and at least one person up top to watch for possible hazards. Radios for communication are a good idea as well if you are belaying your partner from the top of longer routes, especially at rush hour. This warning aside, Rocky Butte has a wide variety of highly enjoyable climbs as well as some great artificial bouldering and top-rope routes in the park above.

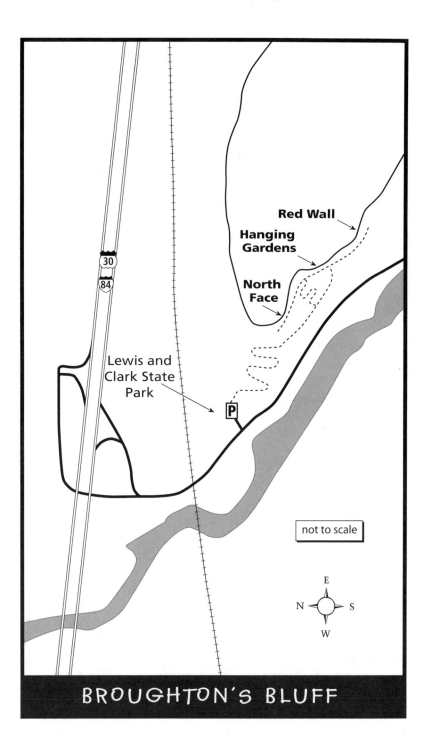

Red Wall

Hanging
Gardens

North
Face

Lewis and
Clark State
Park

P

not to scale

E
N — S
W

BROUGHTON'S BLUFF

Broughton's Bluff

Getting there: Drive east, away from Portland, on I-84 toward Portland Airport/The Dalles, and take exit 18 toward Lewis and Clark State Park/ Oxbow Regional Park. At the stop sign at the end of the exit ramp, turn left onto Crown Point Highway and drive 0.3 mile to a left-hand turn into Lewis and Clark State Park.

Park in the Lewis and Clark State Park parking lot by a grassy field, roughly 30 yards from the trail to the base of the cliff. Gates close at dark year-round. Overflow parking is allowed along the Crown Point Highway approaching the park.

Approach: GPS reading at trailhead, N 45° 32.471' W 122° 22.767'. Trailhead elevation, 537 feet. The trailhead to the climbs is fairly obvious. Walk toward the obvious rock face, and you will see a trail upward consisting of several switchbacks. Stick to the switchbacks to avoid erosion on the path that goes straight up the hillside. After 0.25 mile, you will reach a split in the path.

One option is to head left up a steep trail for 0.15 mile to reach the base of the rock between the North Face (to the left) and the Hanging Gardens Wall (to the right). From here, turn left and hike roughly 50 yards to the base of the North Face, or turn right and round the corner roughly 10 yards to the base of Giant's Staircase. Or, you can also continue up an easy fourth-class scramble to set top ropes on the Hanging Gardens Wall routes.

If you do not take this steeper trail, continue straight another 0.25 mile on a more moderate trail, which meets the rock at the center of the Hanging Gardens Wall. Turn left at the base of the cliff to reach the Hanging Gardens Wall routes, which begin on the far-left corner of this wall. You can also approach the North Face by this second, more moderate trail, by continuing 50 yards past the steep ascent trail on the left and the fourth-class scramble on the right.

The approach from the trailhead takes 15–20 minutes.

NORTH FACE

The North Face is the wall that is visible from I-84. It is the most visually stunning rock face at Broughton's Bluff, with great views of the park and the Sandy River. The routes on this face are fairly exposed and catch sun for a good part of the day. These routes are some of the longest at this area, and they consist of two standard pitches, but climbers often break them into three pitches or skip the final 30- to 40-foot off-width crack.

1. TRAFFIC COURT 5.9 MIXED ★★★

FFA: Wayne Wallace, Robert McGown 1987

The climb begins to the left of the prominent North Face, whose top section is visible from the park below. Climb past a low first bolt through a thin, shallow broken crack in a vertical corner to the left of a blunt arête. Move upward through a dihedral past fixed gear to a stance beneath a bulge. Move up and right over a small roof to join *Gandalf's Grip* at the first-pitch chain anchors. Finish via pitches 2 and 3 of *Gandalf's Grip*. Pro to 2 inches.

2. GANDALF'S GRIP VARIATION 5.9 MIXED ★★

FA: Unknown

This route has the same start as *Traffic Court* to the first low bolt, but then it moves up and right through a thin dihedral, past 1 more bolt, to join *Gandalf's Grip* at its third bolt. Finish as for *Gandalf's Grip* to the same anchors as *Traffic Court* and *Gandalf's Grip*. This variation is slightly easier than the original route, but it is still challenging. Pro to 2 inches.

3. GANDALF'S GRIP 5.9+ MIXED ★★★

FFA: Steve Strauch, John Hack 1968

This is one of the most classic moderate routes at Broughton's Bluff, and although the hardest moves are protected by bolts, its difficulty is not to be underestimated. **Pitch One:** Begin climbing past a low bolt roughly 15 feet to the right of *Traffic Court* and *Gandalf's Grip Variation*. Ascend the flaring, vertical hand-to-finger crack. Move up and left after the crack ends, onto the slab face, balancing on sloping smears past a bolt to a left-facing lieback ledge stance that is protected by a third bolt beneath an overhang. Continue through an overhanging, technical bulge past 1 more bolt, manteling the ledge to chain anchors above. Pro to 3 inches. **Pitch Two:** Follow the obvious crack system straight up past 1 bolt through two slight overhangs, then angle up right to a small ledge beneath an obvious flaring crack. Pro to 3 inches. **Pitch Three:** Climb a flaring crack that is often dirty, through an off-width section at the top to chain anchors. Carry large gear for the top moves. Pro to 4 inches. **Descent:** The descent is a fourth-class scramble between the North Face

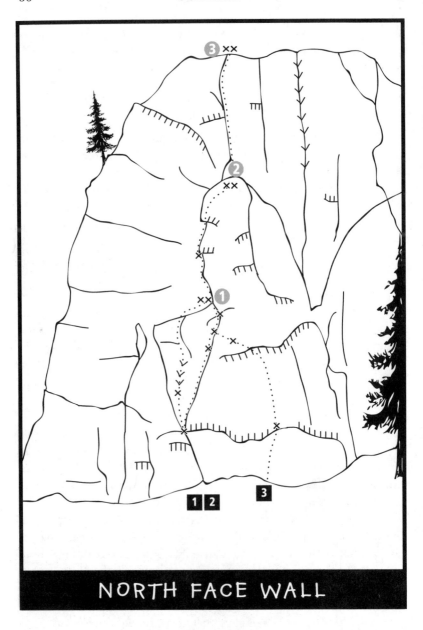

NORTH FACE WALL

and Hanging Gardens Wall or a double-rope rappel to the base of the route. Many climbers skip the third pitch. If you choose to skip it, double-rope rappel to the bottom, or single-rope rappel to the pitch 1 anchors, and then rappel to the bottom from there.

HANGING GARDENS WALL

Hanging Gardens Wall consists of a series of broken columns, with prominent cracks, blocks, and dihedrals. Most single-pitch routes are about 50 feet high, but some go as high as 80 feet, so be sure to check the height before lowering from the top of the climb. This wall is often crowded with groups, as it offers several moderate climbs in a consolidated area. These routes can be easily top roped by scrambling up the gully to the left of *Giant's Staircase*.

Glenda Culbertson navigates the lower cracks of Edges and Ledges.

HANGING GARDENS WALL
(route 1)

1. GIANT'S STAIRCASE 5.6 TRAD ★

FA: Unknown

Located on the far left of Hanging Gardens Wall, this climb looks exactly like it sounds, consisting of blocky, broken dihedrals that stagger up the cliff. There are several cracks to place gear in as you make your way atop small ledges in the basalt columns. This is a common first gear lead for beginning climbers. Save big gear for the top. Bolted belay (watch for loose bolts). Pro to 3½ inches.

2. EDGES AND LEDGES 5.8 MIXED ★★
FA prior to addition of bolts: Jay Kerr
FFA with bolts: Greg Murray, 1992

top not visible

HANGING GARDENS WALL
(route 2)

2

This route starts just to the right of *Giant's Staircase*, moving up two crack systems on columns to the right, using natural pro placements, onto a large, tomahawk-shaped block 30 feet up the cliff. From the top of the

HANGING GARDENS WALL
(routes 3 and 4)

block, the route is protected by bolts. Step out left onto the face and smear on small edges up to the left around a sloping corner. Once the corner is rounded, follow the bolt line to the top. Some loose rock at top. Good intermediate trad/sport lead. Chain anchors. Pro to 2½ inches and 4 bolts.

3. THE SICKLE 5.9 TRAD ★★

FA: Unknown

Originally rated 5.8 in Tim Olson's *Portland Rock Climbs*, this climb requires solid crack climbing through an overhung bulge. Start 15 feet to the right and around the corner from *Edges and Ledges*, to the left of a prominent tree at the base of the rock. Climb up broken columns and dihedral cracks to a ledge stance beneath an off-width crack. Move up left, jamming and liebacking the off-width crack, using stems for balance. Finish right on a finger crack to the top chain anchors. Recommended top rope, especially the first time climbing it. Pro to 4 inches.

4. THE HAMMER 5.8+ TRAD ★★

FA: Unknown

Originally rated 5.7, this route has sandbagged many a climber over the years. Start to the right of *The Sickle*. Climb hand cracks through dihedral columns to a prominent chimney. Move 10 feet through the chimney to a sloped ledge below a crack. Jam the slightly overhung hand crack, moving from left to right. Finish left on a solid horizontal crack system. This route is very challenging for its rating and is not recommended for beginner leaders due to potential ledge fall. Chain anchors. Pro to 3 inches.

RED WALL

This wall is up a short trail that follows the rock to the right of Hanging Gardens Wall. It is redder in color than the other rock, hence the name. You can access this wall by turning right rather than left where the moderate approach trail meets Hanging Gardens Wall. It is often crowded, as top ropes can be set up with a short fourth-class scramble to an exposed ledge above these climbs. This scramble can be protected with natural pro up to the ledge and with quickdraws on anchors along the top. There are several other sets of anchors on this same ledge for top roping. Routes to the left are slab friction and routes to the right are thinner face and dihedral columns.

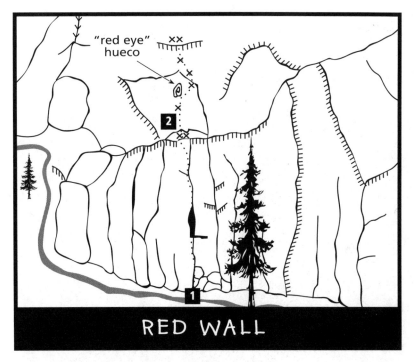

1. CLASSIC CRACK 5.9+ TRAD ★★

FFA: Doug Bower, Dave Cotherin, Robert McGown

While this route feels 5.9+ on top rope, it is a solid 5.10 lead, making it the hardest sustained lead at this area in this guidebook. Start on the prominent vertical crack in the center of Red Wall. Hand and finger jam up a prominent hand and finger crack on the smooth face to the anchor. Top-rope other face routes to left and right from this anchor. This route sees an abundance of traffic and is usually very greasy. Recommended top rope. Pro to 2 inches.

2. RED EYE 5.10b SPORT ★★

FFA: M. Mayko, B. Casey 1976

This is pitch 1 of *Red Eye*. Start at the top anchor for *Classic Crack*. Follow the bolt line straight up through a series of overhangs, past a large, red, eye-shaped hueco, and then back left to chain anchors. This route is short but challenging. 4 bolts.

Opposite: *Michelle New cruises the lower cracks of* Edges *and* Ledges.

Michelle New searches for her next hold near the top of Edges and Ledges.

Carver Bridge Cliffs

Getting there: Drive east, away from Portland, on I-84 toward Portland Airport/The Dalles and merge onto I-205 south via exit 6. Drive for 9 miles, and then take the OR 212 east/OR 224 east exit (exit 12a) toward Clackamas/Estacada. After 0.2 mile, veer right from the off-ramp onto OR 224/OR 212/Clackamas Highway. Continue on this road for 3.2 miles to a stoplight just before an incline, and turn right onto OR 224. Follow this road for 1 mile, and then turn right onto Clackamas River Road. Continue for 0.1 mile, crossing a bridge over the Clackamas River, veering left onto Clackamas River Road/Springwater Road and driving another 0.1 mile. Turn right onto S Hattan Road, following signs to Redland, and drive 0.1 mile. Turn right onto S Gronland Road at the Baker Cabin historical site.

The trail begins behind an iron fence on the right-hand side of the road, 0.1 mile from the intersection of S Hattan Road and S Gronland Road. While some climbers park on the shoulder of the road across S Gronland Road from the Baker Cabin, spaces are limited to two or three cars. If you do choose to park here, be sure not to block driveways, and do not park in the Baker Cabin parking lot.

The recommended parking area is on the left, just before the right-hand turn onto S Hattan Road at the Carver Park Boat Launch. Parking is free during the week, but there is a $3 fee on weekends and holidays (as of May 2006). During the summer, this area is very crowded with swimmers and tubers. Pay attention to signs on the roadway to avoid ticketing or towing. If you have dogs or children, it is best to drop them off with your climbing partner at the trailhead on S Gronland Road and then go park your car at the boat launch, as these residential roads are small and busy.

Approach: GPS reading at trailhead, N 45° 23.326' W 122° 29.855'. From the pullout across from the Baker Cabin, walk a few yards up S Gronland Road, turning right on Stonecliff Drive. This road leads to a gated community above the cliffband.

Walk around the stone wall and gate to an established trail that begins with a wooden footbridge a few yards up on the right. Hike slightly uphill on the single-track trail past several boulders and small rock outcroppings to the left, and up and down some fixed wooden plank stairs. At 0.2 mile the trail forks. Stay right, as the left trail leads to a gate and

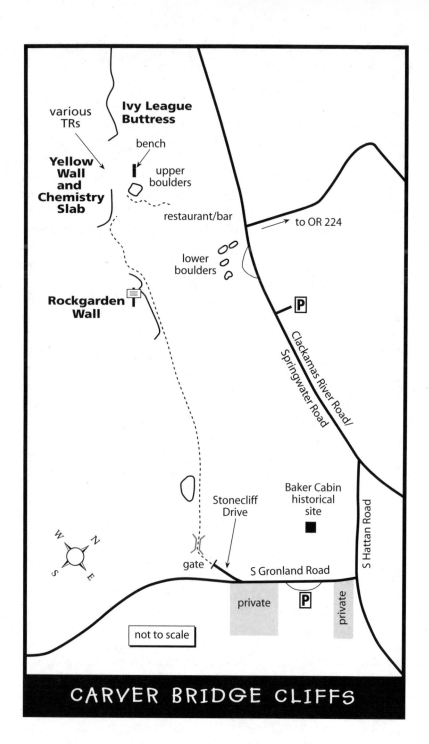

CARVER BRIDGE CLIFFS

private land. After about 75 yards, this main right fork accesses Carver Bridge Cliffs beginning with Rockgarden Wall. The approach from the trailhead takes 10–20 minutes.

In the middle of Rockgarden Wall, there is a trail (not shown on area map) to the right that accesses several upper boulder problems. Pay attention to No Trespassing signs here. There are boulders at the very bottom of the trail as well as just below the cliffband. Do not attempt to access lower boulders via the upper boulder/climbers trail. These lower boulders can be accessed from the first pullout on the right after first turning left onto Clackamas River Road.

There are established benches, and extensive trail maintenance has been done around this area. Again, you must pay a one-time fee and become a member of the Carver Climbing Club to climb here (see Portland Area Beta).

ROCKGARDEN WALL

All climbs at Carver must be led, but some top ropes for harder climbs can be set up by leading an easier climb and traversing over. Rockgarden Wall is the first main wall. All climbs are listed from left to right beginning with *Neptune*, a prominent off-width crack just left of a tree at the base of the rock.

All single-pitch climbs can be top roped with a 60-meter rope. While there are some multipitch routes at Carver, many of the upper climbs are more difficult, so the routes covered in this guide are single pitch. Beware of leading upper pitches without consulting a different guidebook, as the nature of the rock makes some hard climbs look easier than they really are.

1. NEPTUNE 5.9 TRAD
FA: Robert McGown, Tim Olson 1987
Stem and jam up the prominent off-width. Some pro placements are found in the smaller crack to the right of climb. Bolted anchors with webbing are up and right. This climb is hard to protect, so it is not recommended as an introductory 5.9 lead. You can also climb *New Generation* and traverse left, clipping 2 bolts on slab face to set this climb up as a top rope, although this option is challenging as well. Pro to 1½ inches in the small crack or 4+ inches in the larger off-width.

ROCK GARDEN WALL
(route 1)

to anchors

2. NEW GENERATION 5.8+ TRAD ★★

FFA, pitch 1: C. McMullin, Tim Olson 1987

This is the first pitch of *New Generation*. Begin to the right of *Neptune*, just to the right of the tree at the cliff base and to the left of a metal

ROCK GARDEN WALL
(route 2)

to anchors

2

sign about 15 feet up on the wall. Climb the face and crack through a slight flaring overhang. From here move up a finger crack/flake and left to chain anchors. There is a variation that moves right to lower anchors just before the left finger crack traverse. Pro to 2 inches.

to anchors

5.7

5.10

ROCK GARDEN WALL

3

3. SANITY ASSASSIN 5.7 AND 5.10 MIXED ★

FFA: Greg Lyon, Tim Olson 1987

These two short variations are on the detached block about 15 feet right of the metal Carver climbing sign. Either climb the vertical slab face to the first high bolt and then traverse left into the prominent off-width corner with large blocks inside (5.7), or continue up the face past another bolt to chain anchors atop the detached block (5.10). Pro to 4 inches. 2 bolts.

YELLOW WALL AND CHEMISTRY SLAB

From Rockgarden Wall, follow the rock band up a slight incline and then down a slightly steeper slope for 30 yards. The Yellow Wall climbs get shorter as you move down the wall. *Rites of Passage* is a longer route at the beginning of the wall.

Chemistry Slab, a more moderate section of Yellow Wall, begins by the obvious boulder problem beside a wooden plank. There are drill holes at the base of the rock and prominent cracks on either side of the slab. The left crack is *Smooth Operator* and the far-right crack is *Leaning Uncertainty*. There are also several top-rope problems on the wall between these two routes ranging from 5.5 to 5.9.

If you explore the boulders in the woods, be sure to pay attention to No Trespassing signs. Once you see a large building and parking lot downhill, or catch sight of the road, turn back to avoid trespassing.

1. RITES OF PASSAGE
5.10b SPORT ★★
FFA: Tim Olson, Robert McGown 1988

This route is the second bolted climb from the left on Yellow Wall. The climb weaves right to left to right over the course of 80 feet, and routefinding can be tricky at times. Begin on a detached slab, moving

Steve Robson places a high foot in the slab crack on Smooth Operator.

ends on flake with anchors on ledge

YELLOW WALL

right past 1 bolt to a vertical face. Continue moving right past 1 more bolt and then straight up past 2 more bolts and an anchor for a different route to the right. Continue up and left through a slight overhang on thin edges past 2 more bolts to a ledge stance. From the ledge, veer back right past 4 bolts through a prominent flake to the anchor beneath an overhang. Chain anchors. 10 bolts.

2. SMOOTH OPERATOR 5.4 TRAD ★

FA: Unknown

This route accesses the left-side anchors on Chemistry Slab. Begin on the far-left side of the slab, just right of a detached block, following a crack up to a ledge. Move left along the ledge and then up to the left chain anchor on the face above the slab. Pro to 1½ inches.

3. LEANING UNCERTAINTY 5.7 TRAD ★★

FFA: Jeff Alzner, Robert McGown, Mark Simpson

Climb the slab ramp to the far right of Chemistry Slab. Move up and left, placing pro in the hand crack to the right. Move left and then up straight through a blocky section, finishing on face moves to the chain anchor on the right face above the slab. Pro to 4 inches.

CHEMISTRY SLAB
(routes 2 and 3)

IVY LEAGUE BUTTRESS

This wall is just 10 feet around the corner from Chemistry Slab, and you can see the double chain anchors on a tree 40 feet above.

1. RUBICON 5.9 SPORT ★★★

FFA: Tim Olson, G. Lyons 1988

Rubicon has a bouldery start on thin slab face moves. Climbing eases through a series of ledges to an overhanging crux on thin holds. Finish left on a flake to the chain anchors on a tree. This anchor moves, so you may want to carry webbing for a backup anchor on the tree, or bring gear to back it up. 4 bolts, optional pro from 1 to 2 inches in the flake between the last bolt and the anchors.

Rocky Butte

Getting there: Drive east, away from Portland, on I-84 toward Portland Airport/The Dalles. Take exit 5 toward OR 213/82nd Avenue and drive 0.1 mile. Turn right onto NE Multnomah Street and drive 0.1 mile. Then turn right onto NE 82nd Avenue and drive 1.1 miles to the intersection of 82nd Avenue and NE Fremont Street. Turn right onto NE Fremont Street and drive 0.4 mile. Here the road veers left and merges with NE 91st Avenue. After 0.1 mile, the road turns into NE Rocky Butte Road/NE Mason Road. After another 0.1 mile, the road veers around a sharp right corner. The Breakfast Cracks begin on the left-hand side of the road, just after this right-hand turn. Parking is on the left/cliffside shoulder or on the right side of the road for the next 0.3 mile. Do not park at the Bible College; it is private property and trespassing will jeopardize future access at this spot.

Approach: GPS reading at stone guardrail, N 45° 33.032' W 122° 33.892'. The parking pullouts for Rocky Butte are directly above the cliffband. The Rocky Butte areas in this book are described from right to left from the top of the cliff, or left to right from the base of the rock; how you come upon the areas changes depending on the approach trail you use. Approaches take less than 5 minutes for the top of the cliff and 10–25 minutes for the bottom of the cliff.

While rappels are recommended for best access to most climbs, there are several fourth-class descent trails; the loose footing, debris, and bouldery downclimbs make them feel more like easy fifth class however. The descriptions for each area detail the associated anchors and descent trails. Natural landmarks are described for the tops of routes and the belay stations, but routefinding can be difficult from the top. Using radios—having one partner at the top of the cliff and one at the base—will greatly help you navigate this area the first few times you access it.

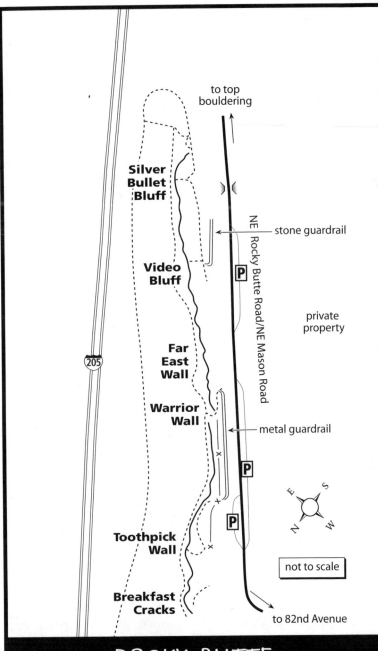

to top
bouldering

Silver Bullet Bluff

stone guardrail

NE Rocky Butte Road/NE Mason Road

P

Video Bluff

private property

Far East Wall

Warrior Wall

metal guardrail

P

P

E S W N

Toothpick Wall

not to scale

Breakfast Cracks

to 82nd Avenue

205

ROCKY BUTTE

There is a wide trail that takes you about 50 yards below the cliffband parallel to the interstate (see the Silver Bullet Bluff approach description). This is the easiest way to hike in, but since this main trail lies so far below the bottom of the cliffband, it can be confusing accessing different walls the first few times you explore the area. Several trails branch off to the left to access various walls, but they are filled with debris, loose rock, and litter. It is recommended to rappel in to each area. While there is a trail that follows the cliffband at the base of the rock, it does not provide easy access to Video Bluff or Far East Wall, as they lie on a higher level of the cliffband than the other areas.

Note also that anchors often change at Rocky Butte, as there is such easy access to the top of the cliffs. Always inspect anchors, and it is not a bad idea to back them up with extra webbing or natural protection. This guide only mentions selected routes along the expansive cliffband. To get a better idea of the area as a whole, visit the website for the American Alpine Club's Oregon section *(http://ors.alpineclub .org/AAC/rocky1.html)*.

SILVER BULLET BLUFF

From the stone guardrail, follow a trail right, passing a tunnel on the right that goes under the roadway. Take the next left trail toward the cliff (continuing straight leads to the trail that parallels the interstate, about 50 yards below the cliffband). At the cliff's edge, scramble down just right of a large tree to an obvious ledge with several chain anchors. Rappel to the base from one of the three sets of anchors. From the base of the cliff, routes are listed from left to right.

1. GUNSMOKE 5.9 TR ★
FFA: Robert McGown, Tim Olson 1987
From the top of the cliff, these are the far-right anchors on the ledge. Face-climb through a series of ledges. Chain anchors.

2. JACK OF HEARTS 5.9+ ★★ TR
FFA: Wayne Wallace, Robert McGown, Tim Olson 1987
From the top of the cliff, these are the far-left anchors on the ledge The route is thin crack climbing on a right-facing corner, through a slab ledge and up a vertical face to the belay ledge. Chain anchors.

to Video Bluff

SILVER BULLET BLUFF

VIDEO BLUFF

Video Bluff is a very popular area for beginners and intermediate climbers, as all routes are easily top roped. The trail just a few feet before the stone guardrail trail leads directly to an exposed dirt patch just above routes 3–5. The trail straight out from the guardrail is above route 1, and the trail in between these two is just above route 2.

There are descent scrambles to both the left and right of this wall, but both require fourth-class to moderate fifth-class downclimbing. Rappeling in from one of the many top anchors is recommended. While many of these climbs could be led, they are generally treated as top-roping problems. Some anchors consist of a few links of chain on 1 or 2 bolts, so bring long webbing or natural protection to back them up. In the spring and after heavy rains, this area stays wet longer than some of the other more vertical walls.

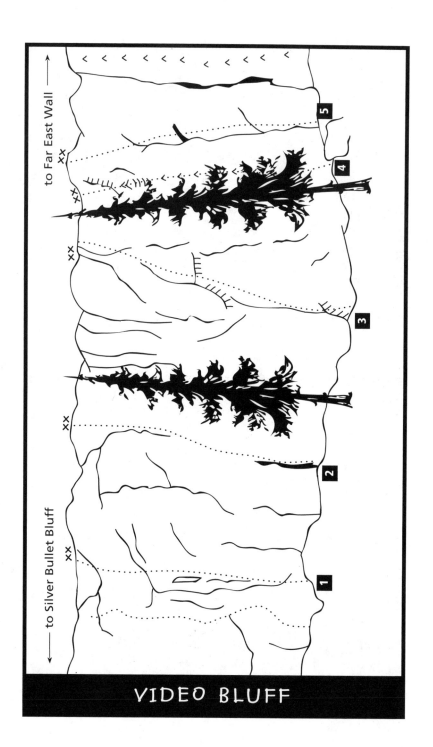

to Far East Wall →

← to Silver Bullet Bluff

VIDEO BLUFF

Heath Knapp smears the basalt face edges of Ace.

1. ACE 5.8 TR ★★

FFA: Tim Olson, Dan Wright 1987

Follow the vertical double crack system up to a small tree ledge. Finish on a slab crack to the ledge. You can do variations using just the right or the left crack. 2 bolts for anchors.

2. ROBOTICS 5.8 TR ★★

FFA: Tim Olson, Dan Wright 1987

This flaring off-width crack tapers to a slab finger crack. The top becomes more of a vertical dihedral, with thin edges on either face. Chain anchors.

3. FLAKEY OLD MAN 5.7 TR ★★

FFA: Tim Olson, Robert McGown 1987

The route begins as slab face climbing to a lieback crack on the left face. Stem right for stability. Watch for loose rock up top. Chain anchors.

4. PANES OF REALITY 5.10a TR ★

FFA: Tim Olson, Robert McGown 1987

This route begins about 12 feet right of *Robotics*, just right of a prominent tree. Friction-climb on thin edges using the bulge, or liebacks to a slab finish. Chain anchors.

5. STAINED GLASS 5.9 TR ★

FFA: Tim Olson, Robert McGown 1987

Climb thin edges on the slab face to the obvious dihedral. Chain anchors.

FAR EAST WALL

The top of this route can be reached by walking toward the rock from the end of the metal guardrail. There are two sets of chain anchors, with a tree for backup. Rappel to reach the base.

1. ORIENT EXPRESS 5.8 SPORT ★★

FFA: M. Pajunas, Rita Hansen, Charlie Martin, G. Rall 1987

Climb the slab dihedral up through a thin crack to chain anchors on the right. You may want to use the tree or a bolt on the route to the left for a directional. 4 bolts.

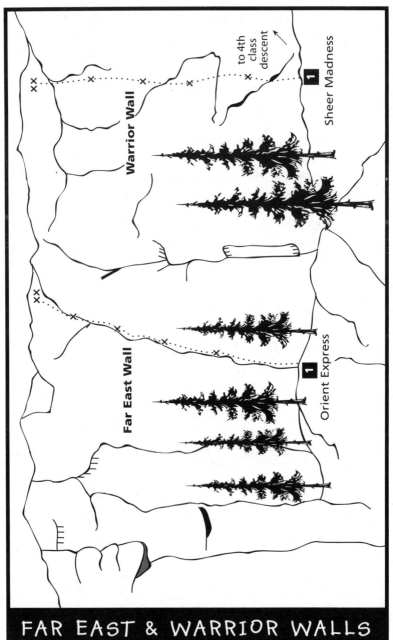

FAR EAST & WARRIOR WALLS

WARRIOR WALL

Take the metal guardrail descent trail to the base of the rock. This trail is loose scree with several exposed sections and bouldery downclimbs. Turn right at the base of the trail. When facing away from the rock, turn right to access Warrior Wall or left to access Toothpick Wall.

1. SHEER MADNESS 5.10a SPORT ★★
FFA: M. Pajunas, J. McCracken 1987

This is the first bolted line on the wall to the right of the base of the trail. Use natural pro to 2 inches in a pocket or stick-clip the first bolt. Climb up the featured face through a bulge just right of the featureless vertical face. Follow bolts up and right to anchors on the face. Do not be misled by a bolt off-route to the left, in between the first and second bolts. Attempting to clip this bolt will take you off-route into a blank section. Chain anchors. 4 bolts.

TOOTHPICK WALL

From above take the trail from the beginning of the fence toward the rock. Straight out leads to a large tree anchor for *Blueberry Jam*. Toward the left, roughly 30 yards, leads to a double tree anchor for *Vertical Therapy*. Rappel to reach the base.

1. BLUEBERRY JAM 5.9+ TRAD ★★★
FA: Robert McGown, Mike Smelsar 1977

This climb starts with a difficult boulder move (5.9+) that seems harder than the route's grade, but it quickly mellows to a 5.9 lieback and jam crack and then climbs onto a low-angle featured face to the top. No fixed anchors. Use long webbing with natural pro and the tree anchor. Pro to 3 inches.

2. VERTICAL THERAPY 5.9 TR ★★
FA: J. Parsley, Dennis Hemminger 1986

Jam the crack to thin face climbing. Resume crack climbing at the top to finish. Back up the tree anchor with natural pro to 3 inches.

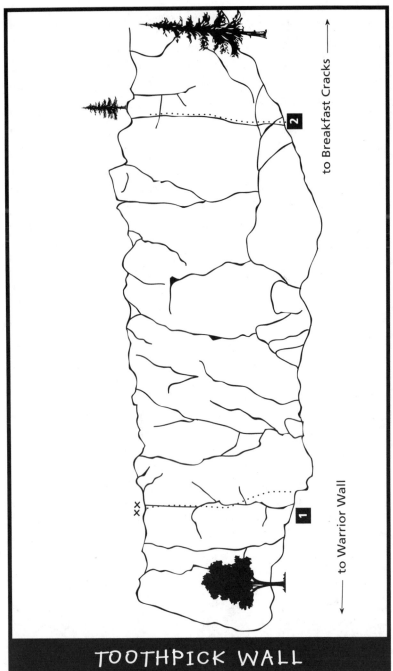

to Breakfast Cracks ——→

←—— to Warrior Wall

TOOTHPICK WALL

BREAKFAST CRACKS

Breakfast Cracks is located just after Rocky Butte Road makes the sharp right-hand turn before the parking pullouts to the left and right. Walk past several large rocks blocking cars from driving to the cliff's edge. This route is directly beneath a tree with chain anchors.

1. EXPRESSO 5.9 TR ★★
FA: Mark Simpson, Rich Warren, Scott Woolums 1977

Climb the dihedral crack through sustained hand and fist jams. The hard exit moves are often dirty. There are chain anchors on a tree. You may want to back up the anchors with long webbing or natural pro to 2 inches.

Mount Hood

For years, much mystery has surrounded rock climbing in the Mount Hood area, and new areas were kept secret as long as possible. While Frenches Dome, Bulo Point, and the Salmon River Slab are all in Tim Olson's *Portland Rock Climbs*, their treatment as adventure climbing areas helps to maintain their shroud of mystery.

Climbing in the Mount Hood area is limited to late spring through early fall due to the altitude of both Frenches Dome and Bulo Point. Both Lolo Pass Road and Forest Road 44 become impassable in the winter months due to snowpack, which generally lasts through early to late April. While the Salmon River Slab is at a lower elevation, rainfall in that area causes seepage on the slab for days after a downpour. Despite these setbacks, all three of these areas have a wide variety of enjoyable climbs in the beginner to intermediate range.

Frenches Dome, the most established of the Mount Hood climbing areas, is located on the western side of the mountain. While this is a relatively small area, it does have several high-quality climbs of varied lengths and difficulties. Frenches Dome is a unique volcanic plug composed of andesite, and the texture of the rock differs from the basalt of Portland. Most established routes are free of loose holds, although you will occasionally come across one, especially when traversing low on the rock. The climbs are often

Andy Bean explores the thin lower face moves of Silver Streak.

covered with a fine layer of dirt, especially early in the season or after a heavy rain. All routes must be led, unless you traverse over from one climb to set up another. You can climb all of the routes in one long day, although you may want to reserve some time to climb *Giant's Staircase* to the summit and negotiate the descent. Stunning views of Mount Hood abound when you reach the top of these routes. Although it is only a stone's throw from the trailhead and road, this area has a wilderness feel to it. In spring 2006, the Forest Service plans to reconstruct belay platforms and fortify the trail to avoid erosion and further loss of natural vegetation in the area. Contact the Zigzag ranger station for full details, and be sure to obey all temporary closures of trails or possibly the entire area during this renovation process (see Mount Hood Beta for contact information).

The Salmon River Slab is a great spot to learn how to sport climb and lead. While the rock is loose in sections and is not as high quality as that at Frenches Dome, it does have an abundance of edges and facial features on slab to near-vertical faces. You can climb all of the routes here in half a day and still have time to take a dip in the river, which this crag overlooks, or to hike the beautiful Salmon River Trail just a few miles down the road. While this is a very small area, it makes up in beauty what it lacks in climbing diversity.

Bulo Point is another little-known gem of the Cascade Range. Located on the northeast side of Mount Hood, the top of this crag overlooks the beginning of the desert that stretches far into eastern Oregon. The rock is andesite, but it resembles the welded tuff of Smith Rock. The majority of routes are south facing, so even at altitude it can get quite warm, especially during the summer. While this area has been climbed sporadically by local Mount Hood and Hood River residents, the majority of bolted lines were developed by Don and Joyce Cossel, Ron Hampton, Mike Richey, Matt Stevens, and Dan Arnold. This area has several established routes, both trad and sport, ranging from 5.6 to 5.12 and varying in height from 30 to 90-plus feet. The surrounding area has several secret spots nearby, but most routes at these areas are more challenging. If you look out on the valley below from the overlook, you can see an abundance of boulders and smaller rock formations scattered throughout the sparse trees for bouldering and top roping.

All three of these area's provide a wide variety of rock type and quality and make for a weekend of exciting adventure climbing with stunning views of Mount Hood, the beautiful Salmon River gorge, and the desert, respectively.

MOUNT HOOD BETA

Drive from Portland ▲ 1–1 1/4 hours

Drive from Eugene ▲ 2 1/2–3 1/2 hours

Drive from Bend ▲ 2–2 1/2 hours

Drive from Pendleton ▲ 3 1/2–4 hours

Approach times ▲ Roadside to 10 minutes

Getting there: Frenches Dome and Salmon River Slab are on the west side of Mount Hood, near Zigzag, and Bulo Point is on the northeast side of the mountain. See the individual areas for driving and trail approach directions.

Time to go: Both Frenches Dome and Bulo Point are over 2000 feet in elevation, so snowpack is a factor. Frenches is more accessible than Bulo, but the best time to go to both areas is between late spring and fall. Roads to Bulo may remain snow-covered through early summer depending on the year's snowfall. The Salmon River Slab is below 2000 feet, but snow and rain still make climbing seasonal.

Rules: All three areas are located in the Mount Hood National Forest, so general Forest Service rules apply. A Northwest Forest Pass is needed for parking at Frenches Dome. There is a ranger station in Zigzag, just before you turn onto Lolo Pass Road (503-622-3191). For more information, visit the Mount Hood National Forest website (*www.fs.fed.us/r6/mthood*) or call the forest headquarters (503-668-1700).

Camping: The closest camping to Frenches Dome is at McNeil and Lost Creek campgrounds on Forest Road 1825. To reach these sites, split right at the fork in Lolo Pass Road, staying low on Forest Road 1828. Then make your first right onto Forest Road 1825. The campgrounds are on the left. You can also camp at the sites near Salmon River Slab, but they are farther away. Free camping for the Salmon River Slab is roughly 1.5 miles past the slab, just beyond a bridge that spans the Salmon River on the left and farther up on the right. There are also established sites at Green Canyon Campground on the right, just before you reach the slab, and at Tollgate Campground, which is on the right side of US 26, 2.5 miles past Lolo Pass Road. Camping for Bulo Point is available at Fifteenmile Campground, just past the intersection of Forest Roads 4420 and 240. There are also campgrounds on Highway 35, just before and just after the turnoff for Forest Road 44.

Food: The town of Sandy, 20 miles west of Lolo Pass Road, has multiple dining options and several grocery stores. Welches is a smaller community located 1 mile west of Lolo Pass Road, and it has several restaurants and a smaller grocery store. Also, 1.5 miles east of Lolo Pass Road is Mount Hood Foods, a grocery/convenience store. For Bulo Point, the town of Parkdale is roughly 15 miles north or the US 35/Forest Road 44 intersection and has a few dining options and a small grocery. Hood River is located roughly 25 miles north of the US 35/Forest Road 44 intersection and has larger grocery stores and multiple dining options.

Climbing type: Frenches Dome consists of face climbing on slab, vertical, and slightly overhung rock. The Salmon River Slab consists of featured face climbing over broken cracks on slab to just under vertical rock. Bulo Point has a mix of face and crack climbing over textured, pocketed rock. Climbs range from slab to vertical to overhung. With the exception of a few trad crack climbs at Bulo Point, the majority of climbing at these areas consists of bolted sport routes. There are top-roping options at Bulo Point, but all routes at Frenches Dome and the Salmon River Slab must be led.

Rock type: Andesite

Gear: 15–20 quickdraws of varied lengths, extra locking carabiners, trad rack to 4 inches with doubles of midsize gear, webbing and runners of various lengths, 60-meter rope (2 ropes for some rappels). Stick-clip for some high bolts at Bulo Point.

Emergency services: Dial 911.

Nearest hospitals: *Frenches Dome/Salmon River Slab:* Legacy Mount Hood Medical Center, 24800 SE Stark Street, Gresham, (503) 667-1122. *Bulo Point:* Providence Hood River Memorial Hospital, 811 13th Street, Hood River, (541) 386-3911 or (800) 955-3911.

Pay phones: *Frenches Dome/Salmon River Slab:* Mount Hood Foods on US 26, 2 miles east of Lolo Pass Road, or Welches Thriftway 1 mile west of Lolo Pass Road. *Bulo Point:* Store on left at intersection of OR 35 and Hood River Highway.

Extras: All areas are dog- and kid-friendly, with established trails. Follow Forest Service rules for pets. Salmon River Slab is close to the road, with the river directly across the street, so keep children and dogs under close watch.

Other local activities: Cycling, fishing, hiking, three ski resorts, backcountry skiing, paddling, and windsurfing.

Frenches Dome

Getting there: Drive east, away from Portland, on I-84 toward Portland Airport/The Dalles, and take the 238th Drive exit (exit 16) toward Wood Village. Over the course of a mile, the road name changes from 238th Drive to 242nd Drive to 242nd Avenue. Roughly 2.5 miles after exiting the interstate, veer left at a major intersection onto NE Burnside Road. Much like the previous road, NE Burnside Road changes names to SE Burnside Street, eventually becoming US 26 east/Mount Hood Highway. Continue on US 26 for 27 miles through the town of Sandy and through the stoplight at Welches to the intersection of US 26 and E Lolo Pass Road. Drive 4.2 miles on E Lolo Pass Road to the Y intersection of Forest Road 18 and Forest Road 1828. Stay straight/left at the fork and continue up Forest Road 18 for 2 miles, and then make a right-hand turn into a small dirt parking area. This is the Frenches Dome trailhead.

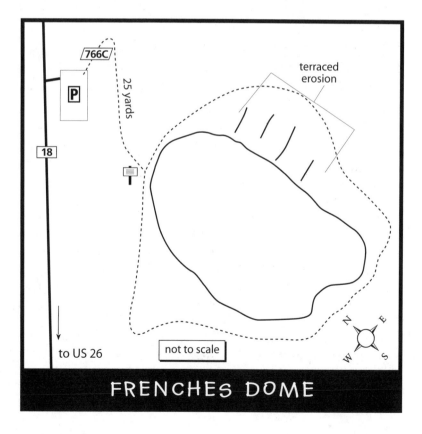

FRENCHES DOME

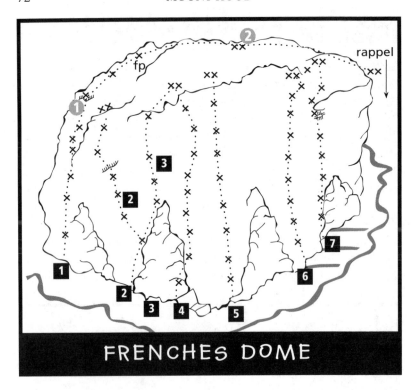

FRENCHES DOME

Approach: GPS reading at trailhead, N 45° 23.873' W 121° 51.608'. Trailhead elevation, 2571 feet. From the parking area, it takes less than 5 minutes to reach these climbs. Descend trail 766c, which heads left and then makes an immediate sharp switchback right. Follow this trail for 25 yards to the base of an 80-foot steep face and a sign. Follow the established trail around right for about 25 more yards to a sharp turn left. Follow this along the base of the wall past an overhanging, featured, yellow ramp to the lowest point on the trail. Just before the trail angles back up and around this free-standing volcanic plug, you will see an obvious blocky, vertical climb to a slab ledge. This is *Giant's Staircase*. Climbs are listed from left to right, starting with *Giant's Staircase*. There is potential for new climbs in between; however, pay close attention to the route descriptions to ensure proper routefinding.

1. GIANT'S STAIRCASE 5.6 SPORT ★★★
FA: Ray Conkling, Leonard Conkling, Keith Petrie 1958
Pitch One: Climb large blocky holds past 3 bolts to a ramp angled up and left. There is one set of anchors to the far left between the third

and fourth bolts. These are not for this climb. Veer right after the third bolt, up the slab to a slight overhanging ledge with blocky holds. Moving right is easier; moving left has smaller holds and is more challenging. There are two sets of anchors above the ledge past the sixth bolt. Use the newer, higher anchors. **Pitch Two:** Climb through a small roof above the anchor and past 1 bolt. Continue up the slab through a series of mossy ledges. The climbing is runout, but becomes fourth class after about 25 feet. Beware of rockfall, as the ledges are covered with loose rock. The last bolt is placed on a horizontal ledge, just above the piton, and often gets covered with gravel. There are 2 bolts spaced about 6 feet apart at the top for an anchor. Bring different lengths of webbing or longer runners to equalize the anchor. 3 bolts and 1 piton. **Descent:** You can double-rope rappel the route, but the abundance of loose rock makes pulling the rope dangerous. Better to do a single, 60-meter-rope rappel from the anchors on the other side of the rock, down the face toward the trailhead and road. Rappeling from these anchors gets you to where the trail first meets the wall. The last 30 feet is a free-hanging rappel, 10 feet out from the wall.

2. TIN TANGLE 5.8 SPORT ★★

FA: Unknown

This climb begins at the lowest point on the wall, just left of a large, mossy ramp, and just right of a smaller mossy rock outcrop. Climb straight up, past 3 bolts to a fourth bolt just beneath a small roof. The moves are slightly overhung, but large holds are abundant. Continue up the blocky rib to the far-left chain anchors on a ledge. Slightly runout and often dirty. 6 bolts.

3. DO IT AGAIN 5.9 SPORT ★

FA: Unknown

This route begins with the first bolt of *Tin Tangle* and then follows a bolt line just right of the overhang and blocky rib. It is generally less dirty and feels slightly easier than *Tin Tangle*, though it is a bit more runout. Finish on large, blocky holds to the same anchor as *Emerald City*. 5 bolts.

4. EMERALD CITY 5.8 SPORT ★★

FA: Unknown

This closely bolted route climbs up and through a blocky outcrop just right of *Do It Again*. Move through edges, side pulls, and jugs to a blocky

Scooter John nearing the anchors on Alpha Centauri

finish left, to the center chain anchors on a ledge about 8 feet right and up from the anchors for *Tin Tangle*. This is the most challenging of the 5.9-and-under sport leads at Frenches. 9 bolts.

5. ALPHA CENTAURI 5.7 SPORT ★★
FA: Unknown

Originally rated 5.8, this closely bolted route is the easiest beginner lead on the wall, as *Giant's Staircase* is more runout. The route starts between two blocky rock outcrops and climbs over the face on slab ledges to an almost vertical finish on positive holds. Use the far-right chain anchors on the ledge, 5 feet right and up from the *Emerald City* anchors. 8 bolts.

6. STRAW MAN 5.8 SPORT ★★

FA: Steve Strauch, Wayne Haack 1970

This is one of the more popular intermediate climbs at Frenches. Climb a slabby face up and left of the slightly overhanging route to the right. *Straw Man* moves up and slightly right before veering left near the top to finish on a blocky slab to chain anchors. One bolt protects the 10-foot traverse between these anchors and the anchors for *Silver Streak*, making it relatively easy to set up a top rope on *Silver Streak*. 9 bolts.

7. SILVER STREAK 5.10b SPORT ★★★

FA: Unknown

The most challenging of the moderate routes on Frenches Dome begins just right of *Straw Man* and just left of the obvious overhanging harder routes. Start on vertical face moves through a pumpy overhanging section. Follow through an overhang and then move left on vertical to low-angle rock. Finish slightly right to chain anchors. You can traverse

Andy Bean makes a crucial clip on his lead ascent of Silver Streak.

over from *Straw Man* and set this up for a top rope. The climbs to the right of this range from 5.11 to hard 5.12. 8 bolts.

Salmon River Slab

Getting there: Drive east, away from Portland, on I-84 toward Portland Airport/The Dalles, and take the 238th Drive exit (exit 16) toward Wood Village. Over the course of a mile, the road name changes from 238th Drive to 242nd Drive to 242nd Avenue. Roughly 2.5 miles after exiting the interstate, veer left at a major intersection onto NE Burnside Road. Much like the previous road, NE Burnside Road changes names to SE Burnside Street, eventually becoming US 26 east/Mount Hood Highway. Continue on US 26 for 26–27 miles through the town of Sandy and through the stoplight at Welches to the intersection of US 26 and Salmon River Road. Turn right onto Salmon River Road and drive 4 miles to the obvious pullout on the left.

Approach: GPS reading at pullout, N 45 deg. 17.528' W 121 deg. 56.578'. Pullout elevation, 2722 feet. The pullout is at the base of the rock. All routes are slab friction and the rock is often wet from drainage. All routes must be led. Traversing is not recommended, as the rock is very loose between climbs. Routes are listed from left to right.

1. UNNAMED 5.7 SPORT ★★
FA: Unknown
This route is the farthest left bolted line on the slab. Follow ledges up and right through a broken crack. Continue through blocky ledges to chain anchors. 6 bolts.

2. UNNAMED 5.9 SPORT ★★★
FA: Unknown
Start on challenging face moves on thin edges and side pulls. Moving right makes for an easier variation. Climb to a horizontal crack beneath a slight overhang onto crisp edges, finishing at chain anchors. 9 bolts.

3. UNNAMED 5.7 SPORT ★
FA: Unknown
Face-climb edges over the slab and bulges to a horizontal crack. Slight runout between bolts 5 and 6. Chain anchors. 8 bolts.

SALMON RIVER SLAB
(routes 1-4)

4. UNNAMED 5.9 SPORT ★

FA: Unknown

Climb sloping edges over a bulge using the arête to the right. Finish on a slab and rounded edges to chain anchors. 6 bolts.

Maureen Pandos leads the far left 5.7 route on the Salmon River Slab.

SALMON RIVER SLAB
(route 5)

5. UNNAMED 5.3 SPORT

FA: Unknown

This climb would be much more fun were it not for loose rock. Move up and left through loose edges over the top of the cave feature. Follow bolts to chain anchors. Feels more like 5.5 than 5.3. 7 bolts.

Bulo Point

Getting there: Drive east, away from Portland, on I-84 toward Portland Airport/The Dalles, and take the 238th Drive exit (exit 16) toward Wood Village. Over the course of a mile, the road name changes from 238th Drive to 242nd Drive to 242nd Avenue. Roughly 2.5 miles after exiting the interstate, veer left at a major intersection onto NE Burnside Road. Much like the previous road, NE Burnside Road changes names to SE Burnside Street, eventually becoming US 26 east/Mount Hood Highway.

Continue on US 26 for 38 miles to Government Camp. Drive another 3 miles on US 26 and then veer right onto US 35 toward Hood River. Continue on US 35, past the White River Sno-Park and Mount Hood Meadows Ski Resort, for roughly 14 miles to the intersection of US 35 and Forest Road 44. This intersection is located between mileposts 71 and 70.

Turn right onto Forest Road 44, and follow this road for 8.6 miles to the intersection with Forest Road 4420 (note that Forest Road 44 makes a sharp right turn at 5.3 miles). Turn right and drive 1.1 miles on Forest Road 4420, following signs to Flag Point. Veer left at Forest Road 4421 and drive 0.15 mile, then stay straight on Forest Road 240 (four-wheel drive recommended). Follow Forest Road 240 for 1 mile through trees, past an open clearing with a sheer drop-off on the driver's side, then up an incline and back into the forest. After 1 mile, there are parking pullouts on both the left and right sides of the road.

Approach: From the small wooded parking area, walk downhill through the trees to a clearing in a boulder field. There are some established problems here, but many of the outcroppings are awkward for climbing, and some landings are bad. The trail forks right just before you reach the first boulders. Veer right to reach the base of the Bulo Point wall, or stay straight for an amazing view northeast to the valley below.

From the trail right to the base, hike downhill for about 25 yards, where the trail veers back left and continues down for another 30–40 yards. You will begin to see short 25- to 30-foot-tall rock outcroppings on your left. Keep hiking another 15 yards and either angle left and uphill for the first gully or stay straight to reach the first main face. The approach takes 5–10 minutes.

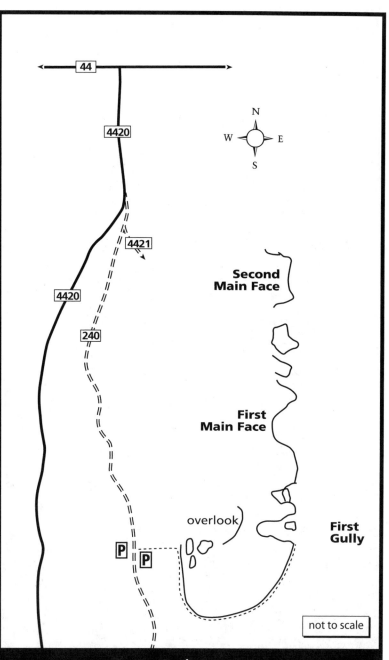

BULO POINT

FIRST GULLY

1. SILENCE OF THE CAMS 5.9 SPORT ★★
FA: Don Cossel, Joyce Cossel 1996

Climb the short overhanging face using edges and side pulls. Finish on ledges and jugs to chain anchors. 3 bolts.

BULO POINT
First Gully
(route 1)

2. INVERSION EXCURSION 5.10a SPORT ★

FA: Mike Richey, Don Cossel 1997

This climb starts at the top of the gully on the right. Climb the off-width crack to vertical face moves at the first bolt. Climb flakes and broken cracks through 2 more bolts on the low-angled featured face. Bolted anchors. 3 bolts.

BULO POINT
First Gully
(route 2)

FIRST MAIN FACE

Pass the first gully and the prominent chockstone gully, which has a rock balanced above its entrance. Walk around the corner to a main wall with two prominent cracks on either side of a slightly overhanging orange face. Routes 1–3 can be top-roped.

Jeff Walker scouts out his next hold on Nuke The Gay Whales For Jesus.

1. PLUMBER'S CRACK 5.6 TRAD ★

FA: Don Cossel, Ron Hampton 1996

Climb through the off-width crack to a blocky ledge. Move left up the off-width, stemming either face. Chain anchors. Pro to 4 inches.

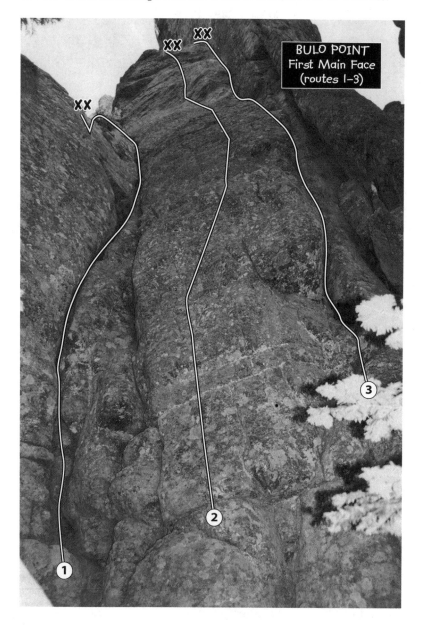

BULO POINT
First Main Face
(routes 1–3)

2. UNNAMED 5.10b/c SPORT ★★★

FA: Unknown

This climb is on a prominent orange face between two crack systems. Climb through edges and ledges at the bottom to a thin edge face. Finish on overhanging ledges to chain anchors. 6 bolts.

BULO POINT
First Main Face
(routes 4 and 5)

3. NOOK AND CRANNY 5.9 TRAD ★

FA: Don Cossel, Ron Hampton 1996

Climb the blocky ledge just right of route 2 to the face. Move right into a slightly off-width hand crack. Chain anchors right of route 2. Pro to 3 inches.

anchors not visible

BULO POINT
First Main Face
(route 6)

4. JET STREAM 5.10a/b SPORT/MIXED ★★★

FA: Matt Stevens, Mike Richey 1996

This is an outstanding longer, sustained climb with a variety of different features and two variations for the finish. Climb the face and the left arête of this pillar on crisp edges and knobs. When you reach the prominent angled crack near the top, move left through the hand crack. This move is a bit runout but can be protected by using pro to 3 inches to a chain anchor left of *Streamline*. Or, as a variation, move right to clip 1 more bolt and finish on the same anchor as *Streamline*. 7 bolts and optional pro to 3 inches, or 8 bolts. Uses a full 60-meter rope.

5. STREAMLINE 5.9 SPORT ★★

FA: Unknown

Clip the same first bolt as *Jet Stream*, then move right to vertical face edges and broken cracks on the right side of the pillar. Climb through a featured bulge to a slightly less than vertical finish on large pockets to chain anchors. 9 bolts. Uses a full 60-meter rope.

6. NUKE THE GAY WHALES FOR JESUS 5.7 SPORT ★★

FA: Unknown

Climb the left side of the second pillar that lies just to the right of *Streamline*. A bouldery start leads to moderate face/arête climbing and then to a large shelf beneath an overhang. There is oftentimes a large bird's nest on this shelf, so be aware. Hand/fist jam the crack through the overhang to moderate slab climbing. Runout at top. Chain anchors. 7 bolts. Uses a full 60-meter rope.

SECOND MAIN FACE

Continue around the corner from First Main Face past an obvious overhanging route to the next main wall, with two sport routes sharing the same anchor. The bolts on both of these lines are roughly 15 feet up.

Opposite: *Matt Bedrin styles the crux of* Scene Of The Crime.

1. SCENE OF THE CRIME 5.10b/c SPORT ★★★

FA: Mike Richey 1996

Make a bouldery start on the far-left side of the rock to a high first bolt. You can protect the first moves with pro to 2 inches. Move right through small ledges and through a juggy overhang to a ledge stance. Climb the featured vertical/slab face to finish. Chain anchors. 5 bolts.

anchors not visible

BULO POINT
Second Main Face
(route 1)

2. DAKIND 5.9 SPORT ★★★

FA: Mike Richey. 1996

DaKind begins about 15 feet to the right of *Scene of the Crime* and has a blocky overhung start and a high first bolt. You can protect beginning moves with pro to 3 inches. Negotiate the overhang onto the vertical/slab face. Finish at the same anchors as *Scene of the Crime*. 6 bolts.

anchors not visible

BULO POINT
Second Main Face
(routes 1 and 2)

Smith Rock

Smith Rock is the most famous climbing area in Oregon. It is a world-class destination, hosting an abundance of climbers of varying nationalities on any given day. The area is popular with all levels of climbers, especially guided groups who can overtake entire walls for hours at a time on busy weekends and holidays. While Smith is known for its challenging sport routes, there are a number of moderates—both traditional and bolted—throughout the park, and they are spaced out enough to leave options open even on the most crowded of days. Smith Rock offers a wide variety of climbing, from thin delicate faces, to cracks, dihedrals, overhangs, and arêtes. The rock on the routes described in this guidebook is welded tuff, and although most routes are relatively clean, there are still loose holds on some of the newly established climbs.

While people were climbing at Smith as early as the 1930s, free climbing did not begin until the 1960s with ascents of such climbs as *Cinnamon Slab, Peking, Lion's Jaw, Spiderman*, and many others not included in this book. Early free-climbing pioneers include Jim Ramsey, Tom and Bob Bauman, Dean Fry, and Jeff Thomas. The level of free climbing moved at a relatively slow pace until the 1970s, which saw free ascents up to the mid-5.11 range. While early pioneers

Maureen Pandos places a high foot while leading Revelations.

looked for routes to summit Smith, ignoring a multitude of shorter routes that ended mid-rock, the climbers of the 1970s and '80s—like Chris Jones—began raising the bar of hard free ascents by employing bouldering methods on some of the steep, overhanging faces lower on the cliff.

With Jones as mentor, Alan Watts, author of the area's main guide-book, *Climber's Guide to Smith Rock*, dismantled early traditionalist ethics by rappeling in from the top of the rock and cleaning loose rock off of some of today's classic sport lines. Starting with unclimbed cracks, he quickly moved to some of the steeper face routes, bolting them on rappel instead of during the climb, the latter being the accepted method of the time. While bolting on rappel was frowned upon by some of the more traditional local climbers, it was an already accepted practice at many areas in the United States and in most of Europe. By employing these innovative methods, Watts raised the bar for route potential at Smith and catapulted Oregon into the world of sport climbing.

In the late 1980s and '90s, the name "Smith Rock" became synony-mous with sport climbing, as it boasted some of the most challenging routes in the world. While new route development slowed toward the end of the 1990s, a new generation of climbers—including Ryan Lawson—continued to establish new lines through the turn of the twenty-first century. With an abundance of unclimbed rock on the back side and other periphery areas, new route potential is still vast within the park. Unlike many areas in the United States, the park department embraces climbing at Smith Rock, and with continued cooperation from climbers and park visitors alike, the sport of rock climbing in Smith Rock State Park should continue to flourish for generations to come.

Smith Rock is such an immense area, it is impossible to include all of the moderate routes in this guidebook. The routes in this chapter were chosen for their accessibility, popularity, safety, and quality. Traditional routes range from 5.5 to 5.9+ and sport climbs from 5.6 to 5.10b. Some very enjoyable routes have been left out to make room for others of the same grade that hold a more classic appeal. This overview of moder-ates at Smith Rock represents a wide range of different climbing styles and encompasses both routes on the front and back of the main rock outcropping. For more information on routes at Smith Rock of all grades, refer to Alan Watts's *Climber's Guide to Smith Rock*, Ryan Lawson's climbing supplement to the Watts guide, and new route information at *www.smithrock.com*.

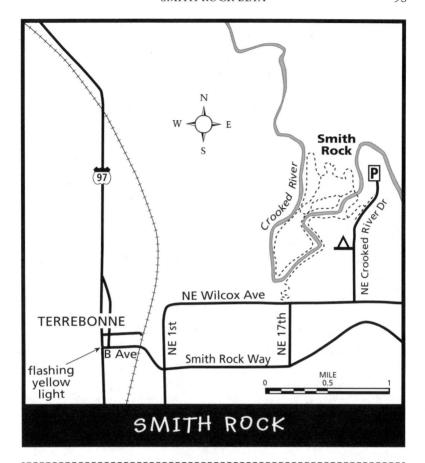

SMITH ROCK

SMITH ROCK BETA

Drive from Portland ▲ 2½–3 hours
Drive from Eugene ▲ 2½–3 hours
Drive from Bend ▲ 35 minutes
Drive from Pendleton ▲ 4–4½ hours
Approach times ▲ 15 minutes to 1 hour

Getting there: From the US 97 intersection in the town of Terrebonne (north of Bend), turn at the flashing yellow light onto B Avenue, which rapidly becomes Smith Rock Way, and drive 0.5 mile. Turn left on NE 1st. The road makes a sharp right-hand turn at 0.4 mile and turns into NE Wilcox Avenue (also called Lambert Road). Continue on NE Wilcox Avenue for 1.3 miles, and then turn left on NE Crooked River Drive, which is also signed as Smith Rock Road (NE 25th Street). Continue on NE Crooked River Drive for 0.5 mile past the Juniper Junction climbing store and the bivouac area to the main parking area on the left.

Time to go: Smith Rock offers year-round climbing, although the heat of summer and the dead of winter are weather dependent. The main season is from March through June and September through November, but weekends anytime and summers can still get crowded depending on the weather. Visit *www.smithrock.com*, the unofficial climbers' website for Smith Rock State Park, which has weather links as well as route info, park info, and a web cam.

Rules: Regulations are posted at the trailhead and are available online at Oregon State Parks, *www.oregon.gov/OPRD/PARKS*. Or you can call the parks department at (541) 548-7501 or the toll-free Portland office number (800) 551-6949. Park only in paved, marked areas. Day-use fee required. As of February 2006 the fee is $3; annual passes are $25 and two-year passes are $40. Stay on open, established trails only. Dogs are allowed only on leashes no more than 6 feet long. Bicycles and horses are allowed on river trails and park roads. No alcoholic beverages. The park is day-use only except in the bivouac area.

Camping: In the park, walk-in camping is allowed only in the bivouac area; no camping in vehicles. The fee is $4 as of February 2006, and this covers the day-use fee as well. The sites are rustic, though there are flush toilets and sinks. Showers are free to campers, but they cost $2 for day-use visitors. Quiet hours are from 10:00 PM to 7:00 AM. There are no open fires allowed in the bivouac area.

There is free camping on nearby BLM land at Skull Hollow, which has pit toilets. From US 97, turn onto Smith Rock Way and follow the road for 4.9 miles to a stop sign at a T in the road. Turn left on Lone Pine Road and follow it for 4.25 miles to the brown BLM Skull Hollow Campground sign. Turn left at the sign onto a gravel road, making another immediate left into the campground.

Food: Terrebonne has only a few food options and one small grocery. There are plenty of food options and larger grocery stores 20 miles north in Madras, 6 miles south in Redmond, and 22 miles south in Bend. Both Redmond and Bend have brewpubs that are quite popular with climbers.

Climbing type: Cracks, columns, and face climbs on slab, vertical, and overhanging rock faces. Trad, mixed, and sport routes. Single-pitch and multipitch options. Most routes need to be led, although Rope de Dope Block has some top-roping opportunities.

Rock type: Welded tuff

Gear: 15–20 quickdraws of varied lengths, extra locking carabiners, trad rack to 4 inches with doubles of midsize gear, webbing and runners of various lengths, 60-meter rope (2 ropes for some rappels). Stick-clip recommended for some high bolts. Dress appropriately, as weather can change quickly. Remember to pack sufficient water, especially in summer.

Emergency services: Dial 911.

Nearest hospital: Central Oregon Community Hospital, 1253 NW Canal Boulevard, Redmond, (541) 548-8131.

Pay phones: Smith Rock's day-use parking area and the Juniper Junction store on the left just before the bivouac area.

Extras: Smith Rock is both kid- and dog-friendly with many well-established trails to explore along the Crooked River. Watch for loose rock and obey all park rules, especially keeping dogs on leashes.

Other local activities: Mountaineering, cycling, paddling, bouldering, fly fishing, and skiing/snowboarding.

Approach: GPS reading at gate at the top parking area, N 44° 22.149' W 121° 07.430'. Trailhead elevation, 2844 feet. From the parking area and fee station, walk north to the main entry trail/access road. Veer left at a gate and descend a paved road, which soon becomes dirt and rock. After about 30 yards, a smaller trail splits to the right toward the visible bridge at the base of the descent. You can either stay straight on the larger trail that winds through switchbacks to the river, or take this right fork, which is the fastest way to the footbridge.

Cross the Crooked River via the footbridge and veer left to access the East Ship (River Face) through the Phoenix Buttress, or ascend the Misery Ridge Trail to the Red Wall and the Smith Summit Trail to the back side. The lower trail to the East Ship (River Face) and the Misery Ridge Trail to the Red Wall form a loop over and around the rock. Be sure to allow 2–3 hours to navigate the full Smith Rock loop; carry a guide or a park map and pay attention to trail signs. You can also access the back side of Smith via Asterisk Pass, but it is recommended to walk around, as it is harder to climb through the pass from the front side than it is from the back. From the parking lot to the footbridge is a 0.75-mile, 10- to 15-minute walk depending on which way you descend.

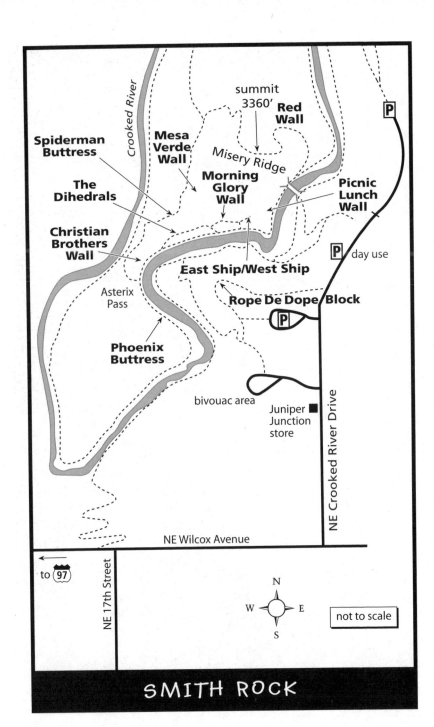

SMITH ROCK

SMITH ROCK

Christian Brothers

The Dihedrals

The Fourth Horseman

The Peanut

Morning Glory Wall

East Ship/ West Ship

to Asterisk Pass

East Ship

After crossing the footbridge, veer left, passing the prominent rock face of Picnic Lunch Wall. After about 50 yards, you will round a bend in the trail and begin to ascend right after another 15 yards onto a subsidiary trail up to the first rock buttress, which is the East Ship/River Face. The approach from the trailhead takes 15–25 minutes.

EAST SHIP
River Face

to Aggro Gully

1. TIME TO SHOWER 5.8 SPORT ★★★

FA: Unknown

Turn right at the base of the rock to reach East Ship. Continue right to a prominent arête. Climb left up the slab ramp to crux moves, rounding an arête to the left. Finish on a featured face slab to the bolted anchor. 5 bolts. Recommended rappel, as lowering on belay creates rope drag.

Molly Grove leads the slab friction face moves of Purple-Headed Warrior.

West Ship

The West Ship begins on the far-left side of Aggro Gully. The following routes are on the smaller rock formations at the base of Aggro Gully, in between the East and West Ships. The approach from the trailhead takes 15–25 minutes.

1. THE PURPLE-HEADED WARRIOR 5.7 SPORT ★★
FA: Unknown

Slab-climb on a variety of knobs and edges to the chain anchors on a ledge. 5 bolts.

2. PHONE CALL FROM SATAN 5.9 SPORT ★★
FA: Unknown

This climb is just left of *The Purple-Headed Warrior*. It has a bouldery start on edges and pockets; then this vertical face finishes with balance moves on a featured slab. Watch for loose rock in the upper sections. Anchors are off-center; bring adjustable runners. Chain anchors. 9 bolts. Uses a full 60-meter rope for rappel.

Morning Glory Wall Area

The Morning Glory Wall Area consists of several walls. From the East and West Ships, follow the cliffband to the left around the corner. From the main lower trail along the river, take the next right-hand trail about 0.2 mile past the East and West Ships trail. Walk up toward the base of the rock past a pit toilet on the left. Veering right from this second trail takes you to the Churning Buttress; veering left takes you to the Zebra Area, the Peanut, the Fourth Horseman, and beyond. Rope de Dope Block lies directly across the river from Morning Glory Wall; it has a different approach trail. The approach to these walls takes 20–30 minutes.

CHURNING BUTTRESS

1. NINE GALLON BUCKETS 5.10b SPORT ★★
FA: Unknown

Pitch One: 5.9 This far-left route on Churning Buttress consists of three short pitches. The first pitch has a bouldery crux move, but quickly progresses into large huecos and pockets to a chain anchor. 4 bolts. **Pitch Two:** 5.10b The second pitch is harder, with a thin crux just beyond the first bolt. Continue up past 3 more bolts to another set of chain anchors. 4 bolts. **Pitch Three:** 5.8+ This short last pitch continues up through easier ground through face edges and pockets to a third set of chain anchors. 2 bolts.

ZEBRA AREA

Continue along the base of the wall past the Overboard Area, which consists of several harder bolted climbs, to the Zebra Area. This wall lies just past a large boulder with a small undercut cave to the left of the trail, and there is a prominent thin bolted dihedral crack called *Zebra/Zion* on the far-right side of this wall.

1. GUMBY/MORNING SKY 5.10b/c SPORT ★★★

FA, Gumby: Alan Watts, Brooke Sandahl 1987
FA, Morning Sky extension: Unknown

This is the second bolted line left from the *Zebra/Zion* dihedral crack. Climb the tricky, thin face past 2 bolts. The original *Gumby* line veered right after these moves to join the last 2 bolts of the harder 5.11 bolted line to the right. The *Morning Sky* extension continues straight up through some large huecos and another section of thin face moves past 7 more bolts to chain anchors. 9 bolts. Uses a full 60-meter rope.

Melinda Kriegh navigates the sea of huecos on Light On The Path.

2. LIGHT ON THE PATH 5.9+ SPORT ★★★

FA: Alan Quine 1988

This is the third bolted line left of the *Zebra/Zion* dihedral crack. The climb is similar to *Gumby*, with easier moves down low. The crux comes high, past the large huecos in the middle of the route. This climb, like many at Smith, has lost some crucial holds over the years, so it feels more like a 5.10 than other 5.9 sport climbs in the park. 8 bolts. Uses a full 60-meter rope for rappel.

3. OUTSIDERS 5.9 SPORT ★★

FA: Ryan Lawson, Holly Beck, Andreas Rossberg

This is the fourth bolted line left from the *Zebra/Zion* dihedral. The route is sustained climbing over a series of edges, pockets, and knobs. 8 bolts. Uses a full 60-meter rope.

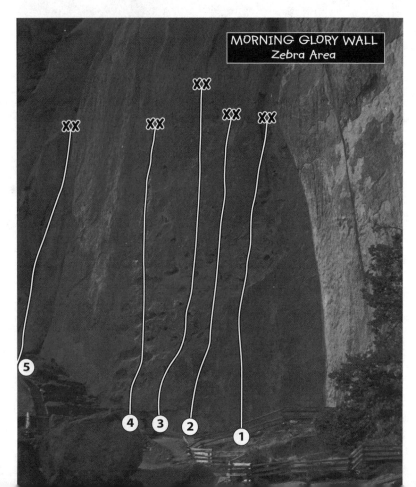

4. FIVE GALLON BUCKETS 5.8 SPORT ★★★

FA: Tom Hinds

This is the fifth bolted line left of the *Zebra/Zion* dihedral. It is a popular warm-up/cool-down route. Follow a series of progressively larger pockets and huecos up to a chain anchor. 7 bolts.

5. LION'S JAW 5.8 TRAD ★★

FA: Tom and Bob Bauman 1967

Round the corner left from *Five Gallon Buckets* and climb this prominent dihedral with a series of stems and jams. This climb is a bit stiff for the 5.8 grade. Although this is a two-pitch climb, the second section is not recommended. Pro to 1½ inches.

Devlin Gonor contemplates her next move while leading Five Gallon Buckets.

Molly Grove stems and jams as she leads the Lion's Jaw *crack.*

THE PEANUT

This detached rock face lies just past the *Lion's Jaw* dihedral. It is aptly named, as it resembles a peanut in its shell.

1. POP GOES THE NUBBIN 5.10a SPORT ★★

FA: Jeff Thomas, Chris Jones 1978

This is the far-right face climb. The route is a thin face, but as the name suggests, it has a series of nubbins along the way. Finish on a 5.6 slab to chain anchors. 7 bolts.

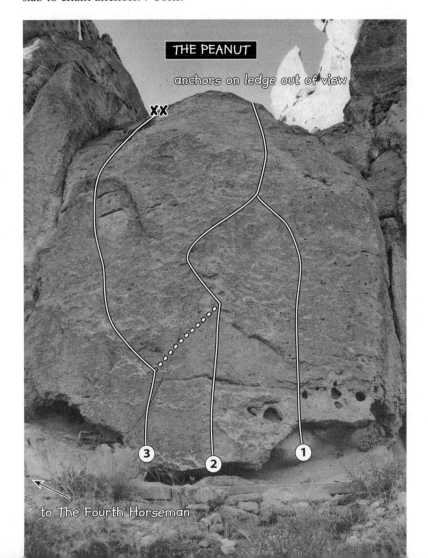

THE PEANUT

anchors on ledge out of view

to The Fourth Horseman

2. PEANUT BRITTLE 5.8 SPORT ★★
FA: Jeff Thomas, Chet Sutterlin 1977

This is the middle bolted line. Start on thin edges to large nubbins, moving left into 5.8 face climbing with nubbins. Finish on the 5.6 slab to the same anchors as *Pop Goes the Nubbin*. The first bolt is high on the route, so a stick-clip is recommended. You can also clip the first bolt on *Hop on Pop*, and then traverse right to this first high bolt. 6 bolts.

3. HOP ON POP 5.8 SPORT ★★★
FA: Alan Watts, JoAnn Miller-Watts 1989

This is the far-left bolted line on the Peanut. It is a good intro-level 5.8 lead with closely spaced bolts. The 5.8 crux is close to the ground. Chain anchors. 6 bolts.

Andrew Ginsberg leads the final moves on Peanut Brittle.

The Fourth Horseman

The Fourth Horseman is the large buttress just left of the Peanut. The following climb follows the lowest point of the Fourth Horseman and does not top out on the actual buttress.

1. SNUFFY SMITH BUTTRESS 5.9 SPORT ★★
FA: Unknown

Located on the far-right side of the Fourth Horseman and just left of the Peanut's *Hop on Pop*. A contrived, brittle beginning is followed by quality rock with sustained climbing. Chain anchors. 7 bolts.

Rope De Dope Block

This block-shaped formation seems small compared to its surroundings. It sits on the opposite side of the river and directly across from the Fourth Horseman. Routes are accessible for top roping from the back side via a short scramble, but there is a tricky boulder problem along this scramble, so it is best to lead *How Low Can You Go* to access the other routes' top-rope anchors.

ROPE DE DOPE BLOCK

Follow the main trail to the river, veering left before you reach the footbridge. Follow the obvious path for roughly 0.3–0.4 mile to a 40- to 50-foot block on the left with a large, flat clearing at the base of the rock. The most noticeable route, *Rope de Dope Crack*, is on the right-hand side of the wall. The approach from the trailhead takes 15–20 minutes.

1. HOW LOW CAN YOU GO 5.6 SPORT ★★
FFA: Alan Watts, JoAnn Miller-Watts 1991

This relatively easy slab with a bouldery start is the second bolted line around the left corner of the Rope de Dope Block. It is a good intro sport lead. 5 bolts.

2. SHAMU 5.9 SPORT ★★
FA: Alan Watts, JoAnn Miller-Watts 1991

This route is just left of the left arête of the Rope de Dope Block; it is roughly 10 feet to the right of *How Low Can You Go*. Climb a series of edges and ledges to chain anchors. 6 bolts.

3. FLOAT LIKE A BUTTERFLY 5.10b SPORT ★★
FA, top rope: Alan Watts 1991

This is one of the more quality climbs on this rock. It starts about 10 feet to the left of the *Rope de Dope Crack* on a challenging face bulge to a high first bolt. Alternate between jugs and side pulls up the center bulge through challenging face moves to chain anchors. Stick-clip recommended. 5 bolts.

4. ROPE DE DOPE CRACK 5.8 TRAD ★★
FA: Unknown

This climb consists of solid crack climbing through a tricky bulge. Solid gear placements, good intermediate gear lead. Chain anchors. Pro to 3 inches.

The Dihedrals

The Dihedrals is one of the most popular climbing areas at Smith, and it can stay crowded for most of the day with groups of beginners. The area begins roughly 0.2 mile past the Fourth Horseman buttress; pass three more prominent buttresses (the other three horsemen), which have fewer established routes. The most prominent feature on the right side of the Dihedrals is the *Cinnamon Slab* route, which follows a prominent hand crack up a slab ramp just right of a thin steep face. The Dihedrals is described in three sections: the right side, the center, and the left side (this order differs from Watts's *Climber's Guide to Smith Rock*). The approach from the trailhead takes 25–35 minutes.

RIGHT SIDE

1. LICHEN IT 5.7 SPORT ★★

FA: Alan Watts, JoAnn Miller-Watts 1989

This is the first bolted line on the right side of the Dihedrals. It is roughly 20–30 feet to the right of the *Cinnamon Slab* crack. This is a good intro to sport leading, with closely spaced bolts. Climb through the vertical face to the 5.6 slab and then up to the chain anchors. 8 bolts.

2. EASY READER 5.6 SPORT ★★

FA: Alan Watts, JoAnn Miller-Watts 1989

This is a great intro sport lead roughly 8 feet to the left of the prominent crack just left of *Lichen It*. Climb the slab face on edges and nubbins. The climbing gets easier higher on the route. Chain anchors. 6 bolts.

3. GINGER SNAP 5.8 SPORT ★★

FA: Alan Watts, JoAnn Miller-Watts 1989

This knobby face is very runout at the beginning. The first bolt is some 25 feet up on the wall, but the climbing to that point is a fourth- to low fifth-class scramble. Start left of *Easy Reader*, and scramble through the broken blocky bottom section to the first bolt just below the slab/vertical face. Continue over knobs and edges to the same pitch 1 belay as *Cinnamon Slab*. 4 bolts.

4. CINNAMON SLAB 5.6 TRAD ★★★

FA: Bob Bauman mid-1960s

This very popular low-grade trad route just left of *Ginger Snap* serves as a test piece for the grade. It is not a recommended first trad lead, as the climbing is sustained throughout the first pitch. **Pitch One:** 5.6 Jam the crack to the left, stemming left, and climb face holds on a ramp to the first belay ledge. There are two sets of anchors here. If you belay from the left anchors, you can see your partner's ascent. Switching belay to the right anchor for the second pitch is recommended, so your belayer can see you. Save large gear for the top to avoid a runout. Multiple good pro placements to 3½ inches. **Pitch Two:** Follow the 5.5 dihedral to the top. A tricky first move is protected by clipping a quickdraw into the far-right anchor. This climb tops out the Dihedrals. There are loose pebbles and scree up top, so beware of rock fall. Pro to 3½ inches. It is a good idea to have doubles of larger gear. **Descent:** This route is tall, so use double 60-meter ropes to rappel to the base, or use one 60-meter rope to rappel to the first belay station and then rappel to the base from there.

CENTER

The center section of the Dihedrals is located farther down the trail from the right side, down two sets of wooden stairs, past a large column with a dihedral to the left of it, and around another corner. One easy way to locate these routes is by passing them and locating the prominent overhanging arête called *Chain Reaction*. From *Chain Reaction*, move right around the corner past two bolted lines to find *Moonshine Dihedral* in the corner. From *Moonshine Dihedral*, continue back right roughly 30 feet to a bolted line just right of an arête. This bolted line is *Wedding Day*.

1. WEDDING DAY 5.10b SPORT ★★

FA: Graeme Aimeer, Grant Davidson 1984

This bolted face lies just right of an arête. Climb tricky knobs and edges using the arête. This route shares anchors with the much harder climb (5.11c) on the left side of the corner. 7 bolts.

2. MOONSHINE DIHEDRAL 5.9 TRAD ★★★

FA, pitch 1: David Jensen, Bob Pierce 1963

This route, located in the dihedral just left of *Wedding Day*, is a test piece for intermediate trad leaders, and it could be one of the most

THE DIHEDRALS
Center
(route 2)

challenging trad leads in this book (comparable to Broughton Bluff's *Gandalf's Grip* at 5.9+). Search for stems to rest on during this incredibly sustained dihedral. Overhung in sections. There is a second 5.9 pitch, but it is not recommended as the rock is loose. Chain anchors. Pro to 3½ inches.

LEFT SIDE
---

1. ANCYLOSTOMA 5.9 SPORT ★★
FA: Brian Baker 1988

This climb is on a detached block just left of the Smith Rock classic *Chain Reaction*. Climb the short detached block. Make face moves on knobs and edges to the bolted anchor. You can use the crack to the left for easier climbing. 3 bolts.

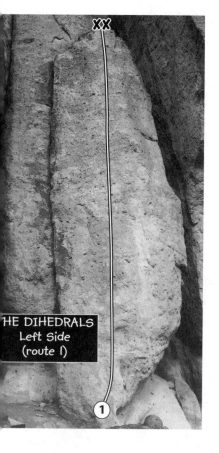

2. BUNNY FACE 5.7 SPORT ★★

FA, pitch 1: Jeff Thomas, Ken Currens 1977
FA, pitch 2: Alan Watts, JoAnn Miller-Watts 1989

This is a very popular multipitch beginner sport lead, to the left of *Ancylostoma*. **Pitch One:** 5.7 Follow a series of large knobs to a bolted belay ledge. Watch out for loose rock up top. Slightly runout to anchors. Chain anchors. 7 bolts. **Pitch Two:** 5.6 Move right, following the slab face to anchors near the top. Chain anchors. 4 bolts. **Descent:** Double 60-meter-rope rappel to base of cliff.

THE DIHEDRALS
Left Side
(routes 2–4)

3. HELIUM WOMAN 5.9 SPORT ★★

FA: Kevin Pogue, Jay Goodwin 1990

The is one of the last routes on the Dihedrals. Follow the right side of the buttress with an early crux. Follow knobs and edges on the face to the anchor. Loose flakes up top. Chain anchors. 8 bolts.

4. CAPTAIN XENOLITH 5.10a SPORT ★★

FA: Kevin Pogue, Jay Goodwin 1991

This is the left bolt line on the same buttress as *Helium Woman*. Small nubbins at the beginning make for a low crux. There are larger knobs and a slab toward the middle of the climb. Bolted anchors. 8 bolts.

Christian Brothers Wall

Located between the Dihedrals and Asterisk Pass, this area houses a variety of quality climbs. It is broken into several areas from left to right. Follow the trail along the cliffband past several hard, overhung sport routes and round a corner. Climbs are described in three areas: The Beard, the Testament Slab Area, and the Combination Blocks Area. The approach from the trailhead takes 30–35 minutes.

CHRISTIAN BROTHERS WALL

Asterisk Pass — Combination Blocks — Testament Slab — The Beard

← to Phoenix Buttress   to the Dihedrals →

THE BEARD

Once you round the corner, the Beard is a highly visible, detached, somewhat triangle-shaped block, roughly 30-feet tall, with crack climbs on either side of it.

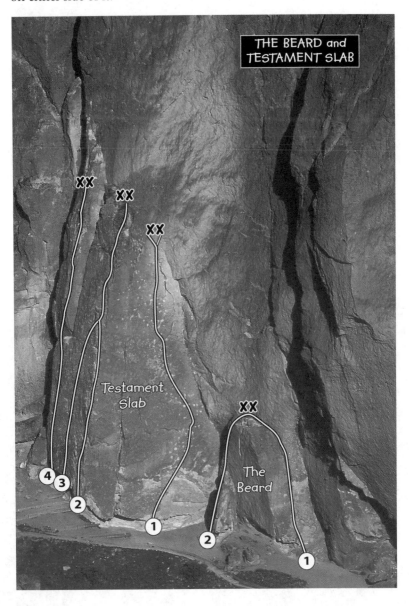

1. THE RIGHT SIDE OF THE BEARD 5.7 TRAD ★★
FA: Tom Bauman, Jan Newman 1968

This is a very short route on a small block in the middle of Christian Brothers Wall. It is a short trad lead, but the sustained climbing may prove challenging for beginners. Climb the thin crack to the right of the Beard formation. The crux comes in the middle of the climb at a bulge. Bolted anchors. Pro to 2 inches.

2. THE LEFT SIDE OF THE BEARD 5.6 TRAD ★★
FA: Tom Bauman, Jan Newman 1968

This is a short route with strong gear placements and is slightly easier than the right-side route. The crux comes at the beginning. Good beginning gear lead. Bolted anchors. Pro to 2½ inches.

TESTAMENT SLAB AREA

This area lies just a few yards down the wall from the Beard, with *Barbeque the Pope* being the first bolted line to the left of that formation.

Maureen Pandos searches for her next hold on Revelations.

1. BARBEQUE THE POPE 5.10b SPORT ★★★

FA: Brooke Sandahl 1987

The first bolt is 15 feet up. You may want to stick-clip it or have bouldering pads beneath you with spotters. Follow obvious thin edges and knobs. Move left after the first bolt for a series of crux moves. Great mid-range 5.10 test piece. Bolted anchors. 7 bolts.

2. REVELATIONS 5.9 SPORT ★★

FA: Tim Carpenter, John Tyreman 1975

Climb the bolted face left of a rounded arête, just left of *Barbeque the Pope*. Using the arête makes the route easier. The first bolt is 20 feet up, but gear to 1½ inches protects the runout. Stick-clip recommended. After the fifth bolt at a ledge, the climbing eases to 5.6. Runout from the last bolt to the anchors. Watch for loose rock at the top. Chain anchors. 7 bolts. Use a 60-meter rope, tie knots in the end, and rappel to the left for safety.

3. IRREVERENCE 5.10a SPORT ★★

FFA: Alan Watts, JoAnn Miller-Watts 1988

Just left of *Revelations*, this line follows small knobs and pockets to meet up with the end of *Revelations*. Although it causes some rope drag, you can clip the fifth bolt on *Revelations* to avoid a runout. Runout from the last bolt to the anchors. Watch for loose rock at the top. 6 or 7 bolts. Uses the same chain anchors as *Revelations*, so use a 60-meter rope and rappel left.

4. NIGHTINGALES ON VACATION 5.10b SPORT ★★

FA: Alan Watts, Amy Bruzzano, JoAnn Miller-Watts 1990

This is the bolted line just left of *Irreverence*. Follow the left arête of the Testament Slab. The route has a 5.8 beginning up 3 bolts to a ledge. Move right to the 5.10 crux at the fourth and fifth bolts to a moderate ending. Well-spaced bolts protect a ledge fall. 7 bolts.

COMBINATION BLOCKS AREA

This area is located farther down the cliff trail toward Asterisk Pass. Continue down the wall past a bolted block with a detached block atop it next to a dihedral. *Lake of Fire* is the third line of bolts from the cave-like dihedral behind this block. These routes are also easy to find by backtracking right from the ascent trail to Asterisk Pass. *Jeté* is the first bolted line from this ascent trail, *Dancer* is the second, and *Lake of Fire* is around the corner to the right of *Dancer*.

1. LAKE OF FIRE 5.10b SPORT ★★

FA: Unknown

This route climbs the face just around the corner right of *Dancer*. It has two crux moves: one at the beginning on small knobs and a second on a slight overhang above a hand crack. Round an arête left to a jug and then finish up a moderate slab to the rightmost anchor on the ledge above *Dancer* and *Jeté*. If you have more than one person follow this route, place a runner as a directional at the move rounding the arête left. Chain anchors. 7 bolts.

2. DANCER 5.7 SPORT ★★★

FA: Tim Carpenter, John Tyreman 1976

Climb knobs through a crux bulge to a slab ending. Good intro sport lead. Traditionally, *Dancer* uses the same left anchors on the ledge as *Jeté*, but you can use the right anchors as well. Chain anchors. 7 bolts.

3. JETÉ 5.8 SPORT ★★

FA: Alan Watts, JoAnn Miller-Watts 1988

This route climbs just left of *Dancer* and shares the same first bolt. Knobby face moves lead to a crux bulge, similar to *Dancer*. Then climb small nubbins on a slab face through a 20-plus-foot runout between the fourth and fifth bolts. Clipping the fifth bolt on *Dancer* eases the runout, but it also makes for rope drag. Meet up with the last 2 bolts of *Dancer* to gain the left anchors on the ledge. This is an intermediate sport lead because of the runout factor. Recommended top rope for beginners, not lead. Chain anchors. 5 bolts.

Phoenix Buttress

Veer left from the cliffband trail just before Asterisk Pass and head toward the main river trail. Turn right when you meet the main river trail and head downstream roughly 50 yards, passing a prominent overhanging, cavelike boulder along the way. Veer right, up the first major side trail, toward a prominent buttress. This area stays shaded for much of the day, so it is a popular summer spot. The approach from the trailhead takes 25–35 minutes.

1. DRILL 'EM AND FILL 'EM 5.10a SPORT ★★
FA: Mike Puddy, Alan Watts 1987

This is the rightmost bolted line on the Phoenix Buttress. Climb past a large, knife-edged flake on the right side of the buttress. Balance on small edges through the crux at the second bolt. Slab-climb on thin

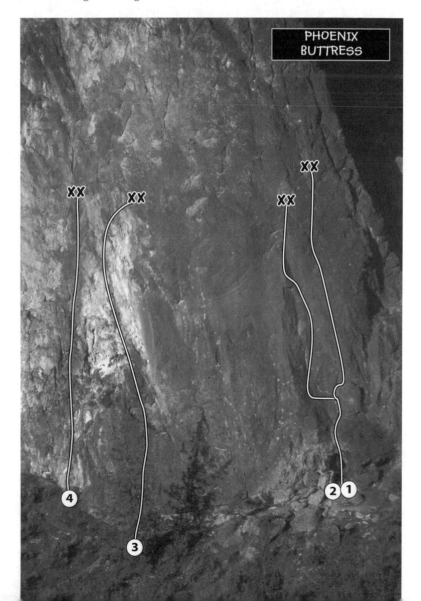

edges to the bolted anchor. A stickclip is recommended or use a large cam to protect climbing to the first bolt. 5 bolts.

2. PHOENIX 5.10a SPORT ★★★

FA: Ken Currens 1976

This is the second bolted line from the right side of the buttress. Climb left of the same detached flake as described in *Drill 'Em and Fill 'Em*. Follow the steep face to the tricky crux, smearing feet high on a thin face. This route is a 5.10a test piece, a must-do route. Use a large cam to protect runout climbing to the first bolt. Chain anchors. 5 bolts.

3. JT'S ROUTE 5.10b SPORT ★★

FA: Unknown

This is the fifth bolted line from the right side of the buttress. Climb large jugs through a dihedral up and left. The route thins out at a rounded bulge to a slab ending. Chain anchors. 7 bolts.

4. HISSING LLAMAS 5.8 SPORT ★★

FA: Unknown

This is the sixth bolted line from the right side of the buttress. Follow a slab ramp up and left using a prominent corner. Chain anchors. 9 bolts.

West Side Crags

These crags can be reached by climbing through Asterisk Pass and rappeling/downclimbing to the western side of Smith Rock, but this way is also harder to navigate, as it consists of fourth- to easy fifth-class downclimbing. Once you descend Asterisk Pass to the west side, follow the cliffband downstream, right if you are facing the river or left if you are facing the rock.

You can also access these routes via the main river trail, continuing around the southern tip until you reach the other side of Asterisk Pass, and then climbing a hillside trail toward the pass. From this west side of Asterisk Pass, continue on the cliff trail downstream between a freestanding rock formation (known as the Awl) and the main cliffband. Continue following this trail until it veers away from the wall for several hundred yards before rejoining the cliffband at the Spiderman Buttress. This approach from the trailhead takes 45 minutes to 1 hour.

SPIDERMAN BUTTRESS

1. SPIDERMAN 5.7 TRAD ★★★

FA: Steve Strauch, Danny Gates 1969

This route follows the right-side crack of the slab buttress at the lowest point on the cliff. It consists of well-protected climbing through two 5.7 pitches and is an area classic. **Pitch One:** 5.7 Climb the hand crack over the slab to a crux bulge and then a bolted belay. Do not mistake the first set of anchors halfway up the first pitch for the end of this section. Chain anchors. Pro to 3 inches. **Pitch Two:** 5.7 Climb the crack up and right to the roof. Lieback around the crux section to a moderate slab finish. Chain anchors. Pro to 3 inches. **Pitch Two variation:** 5.5 Move left from the pitch 1 anchors and follow an easy crack system to the chain anchors left of the *Spiderman* anchors. Pro to 3 inches.

2. OUT OF HARM'S WAY 5.8 MIXED/SPORT ★★
FA: Paul Fry 1988

This is the prominent right side of the flake crack that is just around the corner to the left from *Spiderman*. Climb the right-facing dihedral using the flake crack for gear placements. Meet the first bolted knobby face and climb straight up to the chain anchors. 8 bolts and pro to 1½ inches. Uses a full 60-meter rope.

3. IN HARM'S WAY 5.7 MIXED ★★
FA: Bob Johnson, Doug Phillips 1975

Start as for *Out of Harm's Way*, but do not follow the bolt line right. Continue traversing left to the top of the flake/ledge. Climb through more moderate knobs and pockets to the same anchor as *Out of Harm's Way*. There is a second pitch to this climb, but it is not recommended. Pro to 2 inches. 3 bolts.

MESA VERDE WALL

Just beyond Spiderman Buttress lies Mesa Verde Wall. Once again the trail leaves the cliffband and then meets back up with it again near the base of Mesa Verde Wall. *Screaming Yellow Zonkers* and *Cosmos* are on the

far-left side of the wall, just left of a prominent arête. After these two routes, the cliffband gets smaller and is higher-up on the ridge line. This wall stays shady in the morning during the summer. The approach from the trailhead takes 1–1.5 hours.

1. SCREAMING YELLOW ZONKERS 5.10b SPORT ★★★

FA: Kent Benesch, Alan Watts 1982

This is an excellent intermediate route and a must-lead for any 5.10 sport climbing enthusiast. Climb the vertical face with a variety of knobs. The route begins up and right to the first bolt, but then it angles back left past 4 more bolts. Do not follow the bolt line right past the first bolt, as that route is a 5.10d. At the fifth bolt, the route shifts to the right once more. Quality sustained climbing through the 5.10 crux bulge in the middle of the route. Chain anchors. 12 bolts. Recommended double-rope rappel, as a single 60-meter rap may be too short.

2. COSMOS 5.10a SPORT ★★★

FA: Mike Pajunas, Jon Sprecher, Gary Rall 1989

Cosmos is just left of *Screaming Yellow Zonkers*. Climb the knobby face just right of a prominent arête. Continue up sustained 5.10 climbing past a crux bulge just beneath the chain anchors. 7 bolts. Uses a full 60-meter rope.

RED WALL

The best way to access Red Wall is by following the Misery Ridge Trail directly upward upon crossing the footbridge. Follow the switchbacks uphill and around the right corner of Smith Rock to a relatively level area with several large boulders to the right of the trail. Routes begin here and are listed from left to right. The approach from the trailhead takes 20–30 minutes.

1. DANCES WITH CLAMS 5.10a SPORT ★★

FA: Tom Heins, Pete Keane 1991

This route lies on the right side of a 40- to 50-foot-tall detached flake, just as the Misery Ridge Trail levels out with several boulders to the right of the trail. It is the second fully bolted climb from the far-left side of Red Wall. This is a short but strenuous route with a vertical to overhung pocketed face that climbs to a crux bulge at the top. 4 bolts.

RED WALL
(route 1)

2. SUPER SLAB 5.6 TRAD ★★★

FA: Danny Gates 1969

FFA: Danny Gates, Neal Olsen 1970

To reach *Super Slab*, continue right, past a blank face to a slab corner roughly 0.1 mile uphill from *Dances With Clams*. This is an excellent

anchors not visible

RED WALL
(route 2)

multipitch trad lead on solid rock. The last pitch is the best. **Pitch One:** 5.6 Climb the ramp up and left through a crux bulge to chain anchors at a belay ledge. Pro to 2½ inches. **Pitch Two:** 5.3 Round the corner left to a large ledge, then climb up left through dimples and huecos to a small belay notch. This section consists of easy climbing on runout pro placements. Chain anchors. Pro to 2½ inches. **Pitch Three:** 5.6 Excellent slab crack climbing with solid pro placements. Continue up left on the slab to chain anchors at the top. Pro to 2½ inches. **Descent:** Double-60-meter-rope rappel recommended, instead of climbing up the harder 5.7 slab to the exit gully.

3. LET'S FACE IT 5.10b SPORT ★★

FFA: Tom Egan, Mike Paulson 1988

Continue right along the wall, down a slight decline and around a corner. This prominent bolted face begins to the far-right side of Red Wall, just left around the corner from *Moscow*. Climb the face knobs and edges through challenging moves on quality vertical rock to chain anchors. 6 bolts.

4. MOSCOW 5.6 TRAD ★★★

FA: Pat Callis, Mickey Schurr 1965

Moscow follows the far right of two parallel crack systems to the left side of a corner. This quality, four-pitch climb tops out on the Red Wall summit; it is an exciting and at times challenging multipitch trad route. Start beneath the dihedral. **Pitch One:** 5.6 Climb jugs up a corner to an open-book feature above for a more challenging lead, or work around

RED WALL
(routes 3 and 4)

to anchors

this crux to the left. Climb the face left to chain anchors at a belay ledge. Pro to 3½ inches. **Pitch Two:** 5.6 Climb up and right into a left-facing dihedral. Stem and jam the crack to chain anchors at a belay ledge. Pro to 3½ inches. **Pitch Three:** 5.6 Keep climbing up the corner on a wide slab crack to a low-angle belay ledge and chain anchors. Pro to 3½ inches. **Pitch Four or descent:** Fourth-class slab scramble to the top, or a double-60-meter-rope rappel to the base.

Eugene

While Eugene has never been considered a major destination for climbers, the columns at Skinner Butte have served as a training ground since the 1940s for many notorious Oregon climbing pioneers such as Tom Bauman, Chris Jones, Alan Lester, Bill Ramsey, and Alan Watts among others. Skinner Butte is an urban climbing area much like Rocky Butte in Portland, but it is maintained and regulated by Eugene Parks and Open Spaces, so the area is clean and climbing is much safer. It is an ideal beginner's crag, since all routes can be easily top roped. The drawback of this easy access is that the area can become overcrowded quickly on weekends and weekdays alike.

The rock is composed of closely aligned basalt columns, with a variety of options for face, dihedral, arête, and crack climbing. Most routes range between 40 and 60 feet in height. Skinner Butte is a relatively small climbing area, but that has not stopped local climbers from developing over seventy variations to what would make up about ten to fifteen climbs at any other area in the state. To make this many climbs, strict rules apply as to which holds can be used and which ones are off-limits. In that aspect, this area has an outdoor gymlike feel to it. The city of Eugene moved to preserve the history and accessibility of Skinner Butte by making it a climbing park in 1975. Due to shifts in the rock, the far-right side of the

Chris Smith stems the middle section of The Hydrotube's *first pitch.*

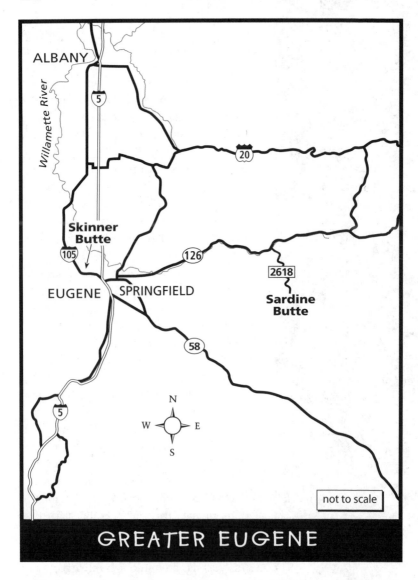

GREATER EUGENE

columns have become unstable and are closed. Please pay attention to closures to preserve access to this unique park.

In the western Cascades, one hour east of Eugene, is Flagstone, a large dome formation with excellent slab climbing as well as vertical and overhung features. The summit of Flagstone is 4100 feet high. Early pioneers of Flagstone were Alan Amos and Mark Ashworth, who first ascended the dome via *Acne Problem* 5.7/5.8, just left of the famous *Hydrotube*. Climbers such as Walt Covington (who completed the first full free ascent of *The Hydrotube*) and the Tvedt family contributed to more sport route development during the early to mid-1990s. Routes cover three-quarters of the circumference of the rock, with moderate climbs on the two slab faces to the left of the Great White Wall (the first wall the trail comes to) and two more-vertical walls to the right.

The drive to Flagstone is enjoyable, as it winds along the scenic McKenzie River. Both areas offer an abundance of climbs in a variety of styles for both beginner and intermediate climbers. Join the likes of some of Oregon's greatest climbers by practicing your moves at Skinner Butte before plying them on the longer faces of Flagstone.

EUGENE AREA BETA

Drive from Portland	▲	2–3 hours
Drive from Seattle	▲	5–6 hours
Drive from Bend	▲	2 1/2–3 hours
Drive from Pendleton	▲	5 1/2–6 1/2 hours
Approach times	▲	Roadside to 5–10 minutes

Getting there: Skinner Butte is in Eugene, just off I-105 by the Willamette River, about 12–15 blocks northeast of the fairgrounds; and Flagstone is east of Eugene. See the individual areas for driving and trail approach directions.

Time to go: While the weather in Eugene is slightly drier than Portland, the climbing season is still predominately from late spring to fall. Year-round climbing is possible, but weather is a factor, especially at Flagstone, which is at 4100 feet and gets snowed-in during winter and early spring.

Rules: Skinner Butte is a city park, so Eugene Parks and Open Space rules apply. Visit the department's website at *www.ci.eugene.or.us/pw/parks* or call (541) 682-4800. Flagstone is located just within the Willamette National Forest and Forest Service rules apply. Visit the national forest's website at *www.fs.fed.us/r6/willamette*, or call the McKenzie River Ranger District at (541)-822-3381 or the Willamette National Forest Supervisor's Office at (541)-225-6300.

Camping: There are no campgrounds in Eugene proper for Skinner Butte, but there are multiple hotel options. You can also drive east along the McKenzie River to campgrounds along OR 126. For Flagstone, there are several campgrounds east on OR 126 near the towns of Blue River and McKenzie Bridge. See details at the Willamette National Forest's website, listed above.

Food: There are plenty of food options, including fast food, restaurants, and grocery stores, in the greater Springfield/Eugene metropolitan area, some within walking distance of Skinner Butte. For Flagstone, the closest food and convenience store is the Finn Rock Store on OR 126 east, just past the turnoff for Quartz Creek Road. Other options include driving east on OR 126 to the town of Blue River, or west to the town of Vida.

Climbing type: Skinner Butte has top roping and trad crack and face climbing on basalt columns. Flagstone has a wide range of sport climbs on rock faces ranging from slab to vertical to overhung.

Rock type: Basalt at Skinner Butte; andesite at Flagstone.

Gear: 15–20 quickdraws of varied lengths, extra locking carabiners, trad rack to 4 inches with doubles of midsize gear, webbing and runners of various lengths, 60-meter rope (2 ropes for some rappels at Flagstone).

Emergency services: Dial 911.

Nearest hospitals: *Skinner Butte*: Sacred Heart Medical Center,1255 Hilyard Street, Eugene, (541) 686-7300. *Flagstone:* McKenzie Willamette Hospital, 1460 G Street, Springfield, (541) 726-4400.

Pay phones: *Skinner Butte:* Crux Climbing Gym or REI, both on W 3rd Avenue. *Flagstone:* Finn Rock Store on OR 126 east.

Extras: Both areas are dog- and kid-friendly. For Skinner Butte, follow Eugene Parks and Open Space rules (dogs on leash). For Flagstone, follow Forest Service rules for dogs. Flagstone is not ideal for children or pets if you are doing multipitch routes, unless you have someone to watch your child or pet while you negotiate your ascent and descent. The Willamette River is near Skinner Butte, and Quartz Creek and the McKenzie River are near Flagstone.

Other local activities: Cycling, hiking, fishing, paddling, and indoor climbing at Crux Rock Gym on W 3rd Avenue.

Skinner Butte

Getting there: From I-5 near Eugene, take I-105 west/OR 126 west via exit 194b toward Eugene. Drive 3.3 miles to the OR 99 south/Jefferson Street exit on the left, which goes toward the City Center Mall/fairgrounds. At the end of the off-ramp, turn left onto W 7th Avenue/OR 99 south. Drive 0.1 mile, and then turn left onto Lincoln Street and follow it across railroad tracks to the parking area under the Skinner Butte columns.

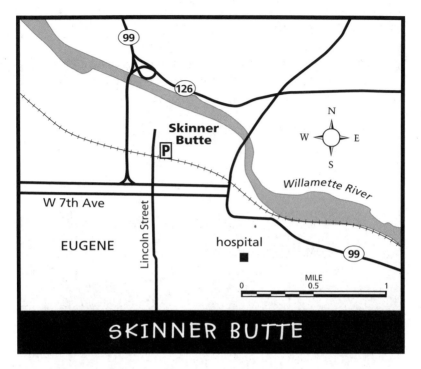

Approach: Park in the designated area directly in front of the climbs. A fourth-class scramble to the far left of the cliff accesses top-rope anchors. All routes can be top roped, although some of the far-right climbs require downclimbing on loose terrain to access the anchors.

WILDERNESS WALL

Routes move from left to right on the columns, with the first two being 5.6 access routes to the first anchor. Accessing the top using one of these routes is a cleaner option than the fourth-class scramble. Although most of these climbs can be led with a standard rack of traditional gear with double camming units in midrange sizes, they are generally top roped.

1. TRANSPORTATION ROUTES 5.6 TR
FA: Unknown
Climb through a series of blocky dihedrals and ledges to access the top of the cliff. One route is far left and the other is 5 feet to the right of it.

2. UNNAMED 5.8 TR ★★

FA: Unknown

This climb starts on a cluster of broken columns about 15 feet to the right of *Transportation Routes*. For the 5.8 rating, climb the face of the column using only face holds and the right edge.

3. WEIRD LIEBACK 5.9+ TR ★

FA: Unknown

Climb to the right up blocky columns into a dihedral. Climb the face of the column for a 5.9 rating, or use the crack to make the climb easier.

NEW CHIMNEY
----

1. NEW CHIMNEY 5.8 TR ★
FA: Unknown

This route is named after a new chimney that was formed when one of the columns fell out in 1969. Climb the obvious chimney using all available holds.

2. BAT CRACK 5.7 TR ★
FA: Pat Callis 1960s

Follow the dihedral crack between two columns. Begins as an off-width, turning into a hand crack higher up. Chain anchors.

MAIN BUTTRESS

Columns on the Main Buttress are numbered, moving from fifth to first as you go left to right along the wall.

1. FIFTH COLUMN/SIGN FACE 5.10a TR ★
FA: Pat Callis 1960s

Face-climb this column using the edges on both sides. It begins on big blocks, but gets thinner higher up. Chain anchors.

2. FOURTH COLUMN 5.7 TR ★
FA: Unknown

Climb the face of the fourth column using finger/hand cracks to the left and right. Use same anchors as *Fifth Column/Sign Face* or *Forthright*. May need to set directional with natural pro.

3. FORTHRIGHT 5.9 TR ★★
FA: Wayne Arrington, Mike Seeley 1970s

Climb the right-side crack of the fourth column using only the crack and right face holds. Chain anchors.

4. THIRD COLUMN/BARN DOOR LIEBACK 5.8 TR ★
FA: Unknown

Using either the arête or the face, negotiate the third column with a series of liebacks. Good practice for using body tension to hold on. Use same anchors as *Forthright*.

5. SECOND COLUMN 5.8 TR ★

FA: Unknown

Face-climb the second column using the cracks on either side. Try a 5.8 variation using only the left crack and face holds or a 5.10 variation using the right crack and face holds. Chain anchors.

MAIN CHIMNEY WALL

1. MAIN CHIMNEY 5.7 TR ★
FA: Unknown

Negotiate the main chimney by jamming and stemming. Chain anchors.

2. RIGHT SKI TRACK 5.10a TR ★

FA: Unknown

This is the second main crack to the right of *Main Chimney*. Jam and smear up, using only the right crack, to chain anchors.

3. GRASS CRACK 5.9 TR ★

FA: Unknown

This is the prominent crack one column right of *Right Ski Track*. Use the crack and column face for feet and hands. Chain anchors.

Brian Bauer nears the final moves of Grass Crack.

OUTER COLUMN
----

1. OUTER COLUMN JAM 5.8 TR ★★
FA: Tom Bauman 1960s
Climb using hand and foot jams in the crack. There are good edges on either side of the crack. Chain anchors. Recommended rappel, as rope may stick in the crack.

2. HARD LIEBACK 5.10a TR ★★
FA: Tom Rogers 1970s
Use the crack and either side's face holds to anchor.

ETUDES
----

1. LIMPDICK 5.10b/c TR ★★★
FA: Wayne Arrington 1972
This local classic is the last crack in the open portion of the columns. Do not stem too far or you will be in the off-limits section. Negotiate the crack with finger to hand jams, using the main face and crack for feet.

Flagstone

Getting there: From I-5 near Eugene, take OR 126 east via exit 194 and stay on this road for 38 miles through the city of Springfield. Shortly after you leave Springfield, the road begins to wind along the McKenzie River. Continue through the towns of Leaburg, Vida, and Nimrod to the intersection of OR 126 east and Quartz Creek Road/Forest Road 2618.

Reset your odometer and turn right, crossing the McKenzie River. Drive 10.8 miles and then veer right at a fork in the road. Turn left at 13 miles (this road is still Forest Road 2618). Turn right onto Forest Road 350 at 14 miles. Continue for 0.2 mile and park on the right-hand shoulder at a small pullout.

Approach: From the pullout, cross the road and climb the trail 25 yards to the base of Great White Wall. Veer right and round the corner past Center Wall to reach Hydrotube Wall and Walt's Wall, or veer left to reach North Corner.

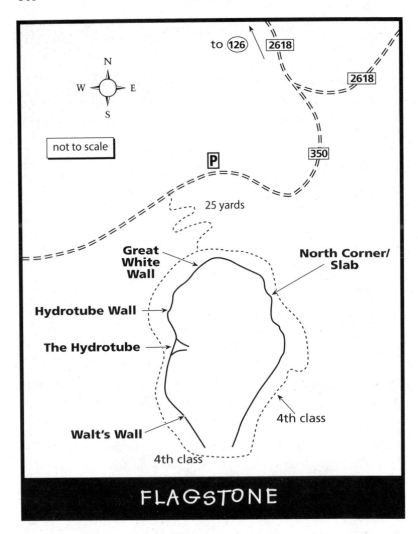

HYDROTUBE WALL

This wall begins just as you round the corner from the Center Wall. Walk uphill until you see the prominent *Hydrotube* feature to the left. This area can be confusing to navigate at first, as there are an abundance of bolts that branch out from other routes. The routes are listed from left to right. Although the upper portions of *Clearasil* and *Scarface* (routes 2 and 3) lie to the left of *Acne Problem* (route 1), they share the same start with this classic route, so their descriptions follow *Acne Problem*.

FLAGSTONE
Hydrotube Wall
(routes 1–4)

1. ACNE PROBLEM 5.7+ SPORT ★★★

FA: Alan Amos, Mark Ashworth 1986

Begin just left of the obvious *Hydrotube* feature with a strenuous
lieback start, using underclings and side pulls to a featured face. This

Hunter Lipscomb balances his way through the delicate entry moves of Acne Problem.

route moves up and left. There is a newer climb that stays on the arête between *The Hydrotube* and *Acne Problem*, sharing the first 2 bolts and the last 2 bolts of *Acne Problem* (7 bolts total). It is a bit harder, more runout, and relatively contrived. *Acne Problem* shares anchors with *The Hydrotube* and uses a full 60-meter rope for rappel. 9 bolts.

2. CLEARASIL 5.10a/b
SPORT ★★

FA: Alan Amos, Mark Ashworth 1996

Pitch One: This climb shares the first 3 bolts with *Acne Problem*. It then moves left onto steeper slab/vertical face moves to chain anchors on the face down and left of the *Acne Problem/Hydrotube* anchor ledge. 9 bolts. **Pitch Two:** This pitch moves up and left through featured slab/vertical rock to finish at the same anchors as *Scarface*. 5 bolts. **Descent:** Descend as for *Scarface*.

3. SCARFACE 5.8+
SPORT ★★

FA: Alan Amos 1987

Start as for *Acne Problem*, but veer up and about 10 feet left after the first bolt. Pass the first-pitch

Matt Bedrin works through the final moves of The Hydrotube's *first pitch.*

anchor of *Clearasil*, and continue climbing to *Clearasil's* second-pitch anchors. Walk off, double-rope rappel, or single-rope rappel to *Clearasil's* first-pitch anchors and then down from there. 16 bolts.

4. THE HYDROTUBE 5.9 SPORT ★★★

FA, pitch 1: Walt Corvington, Alan Amos 1989
FA, pitch 2: Walt Corvington 1990

This remarkable feature resembles a shallow, rounded dihedral. **Pitch One:** 5.9 Stick-clip the high first bolt or protect climbing with pro to 2½ inches. Stem on small edges and smears using flakes to the right. Move left at the top to a ledge. This is a full 60-meter-rope rappel, so if you rappel from here make sure your ends are even, knotted, and on the ground. Chain anchors. 9 bolts. **Pitch Two:** 5.6 Runout. Move right off of the ledge on the featured and pocketed slab face. Chain anchors. 4 bolts. **Descent:** Walk off or double-rope rappel to the bottom. There is a way to single-rope rappel to lower anchors for a different route not described here and then down to the base from there. This option can be confusing the first time you attempt it, so a double-rope rappel or walk-off is recommended.

FLAGSTONE
Hydrotube Wall
(routes 4 and 5)

to **1** anchors

5

start of route not visible

4

5. GAMES WITHOUT FRONTIERS 5.10b SPORT ★★★

FA: Dave and Jean Reinhart-Trepp 1991

This is the third bolted line to the right of *The Hydrotube*; the first line right shares the same first bolt as *The Hydrotube* and then branches off right. Climb a ramp up past 3 bolts and around an overhanging arête to the right. Continue on the vertical face and overhung ledges to the top chain anchors. 8 bolts. Uses a full 60-meter rope.

WALT'S WALL

Continue around the right side from *The Hydrotube* and move up a slight incline. Routes begin about 15 feet around the corner from *Games Without Frontiers*.

1. AFTERNOON DELIGHT 5.8 SPORT ★

FA: Walt Corvington, Alan Amos 1989

This second bolted line over from *Games Without Frontiers* has a thin, balancey start through 3 bolts and then moves right to a small, sloping ramp and a double set of chain anchors. Use the left anchors for this climb and the right anchors for *Morning Desire*. Staying left of the bolt line makes this climb harder. There is also a harder 5.9+ variation that goes straight after the fourth bolt through 3 more bolts to single chain anchors on the left. 6 bolts.

2. MORNING DESIRE 5.10a SPORT ★★

FA: Walt Corvington 1990

Face-climb thin edges up and left through 4 bolts, then join *Afternoon Delight* up the small, sloping ramp to the right chain anchors. 7 bolts.

3. DEEP POCKETS 5.9 SPORT ★★★

FA: Mark Ashworth, Alan Amos 1994

This is the last route on the far right of the wall before the trail angles away from the rock and then scrambles up to the top. Make a bouldery start through pockets and edges to larger huecos. There are two cruxes, one low on the route and one in the middle. The route moves up and right to finish on a low-angle pocketed face. Chain anchors. Bolts. Single-rope rappel.

FLAGSTONE
Walt's Wall
(routes 1 and 2)

anchors not visible

FLAGSTONE
Walt's Wall
(route 3)

③

NORTH CORNER/SLAB

To reach North Corner, veer left at the Great White Wall instead of veering right to *The Hydrotube*. Round the corner, and after about 20 yards, climbs begin from right to left, or downhill to uphill. This wall has an abundance of climbs, and most of them are very closely bolted.

1. TOY BOX 5.8 SPORT ★★

FA: Walt Corvington, Dianne Cornett, Larry Modrell 1990

This is the first climb on North Corner. **Pitch One:** Climb the slab past a bulge over the friction face to chain anchors. This pitch is just over 100 feet. You can top-rope with a 60-meter rope if the belayer stands

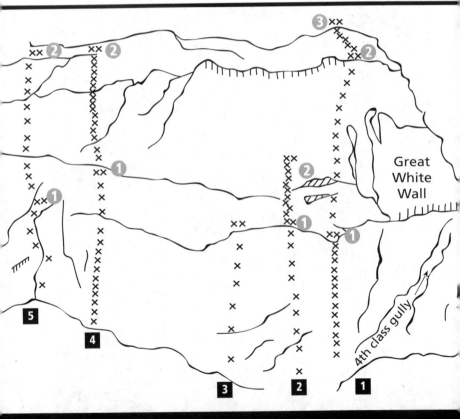

FLAGSTONE: NORTH CORNER

higher left up the trail. 13 bolts. When rappeling from pitch 1, be sure to tie knots in the end of your rope for safety. **Pitch Two:** 5.8 Climb over a slight bulge onto the upper slab and make friction moves to chain anchors. Thin friction moves make this pitch seem harder than 5.8. 11 bolts. This pitch is a full 60-meter rappel as well. **Pitch Three:** 5.6 Balance on slab friction holds directly up from the belay. Chain anchors. 5 bolts. **Descent:** Rappel to pitch 2 anchors, then down to pitch 1 anchors, then to the ground. Pay attention to descent safety instructions in the pitch 1 and 2 descriptions.

2. ONCE UPON A TIME 5.6 SPORT ★★

FA: David and Dee Tvedt 2000

Closely spaced bolts and relative ease for the grade make this a good beginner multipitch lead. **Pitch One:** Friction-climb the low-angle slab. Chain anchors. 9 bolts. **Pitch Two:** Continue through a slight overhang to chain anchors. 8 bolts. **Descent:** Double-rope rappel to the bottom, or single 60-meter-rope rappel each pitch.

3. THE LOST OXYMORON 5.7 SPORT ★★

FA: David and Dee Tvedt 2000

Make slab friction moves over smooth holds. Chain anchors. 6 bolts.

4. NORTHERN LIGHTS 5.9 SPORT ★★★

FA, pitch 1: Keenan, Dee, and David Tvedt 2000
FA, pitch 2: Dee and David Tvedt 2000

Pitch One: 5.8 Climb the slab face through vertical thin friction moves to chain anchors. Feels more like 5.6 with a 5.8 crux high on the route. 14 bolts. **Pitch Two:** This is solid 5.9 friction/face climbing over a long pitch. 15 bolts. **Descent:** You can double-rope rappel to the bottom, or do a full 60-meter-rope rappel to the first-pitch anchor and then down from there. Be sure your rope is even with knotted ends.

5. PYGMY TWILIGHT 5.8 SPORT ★★

FA: Mark Ashworth, Steve Cuddeback 1994

Pitch One: 5.5 Low-angled slab climbing. Chain anchors. 5 bolts. **Pitch Two:** 5.8 Slab friction-climb to vertical face smears on sparse holds. The friction crux is near the top of the route. Chain anchors. 10 bolts. **Descent:** Double-rope rappel, or do a full 60-meter-rope rappel to the first anchor and then down from there.

The Callahans

Nestled nearly 2000 feet high on a hillside above the Flournoy Valley, west of Roseburg, the Callahans consist of a series of sandstone cliffs scattered throughout the woods just below Reston Ridge. Various rock formations stretch for several miles along the access road atop the cliff, which is owned and maintained by Weyerhaeuser. Be sure to obey all rules listed in the Callahans Beta to maintain future access to these cliffs.

Climbers began exploring these rocks in the mid-1980s, establishing mostly traditional lines as the methods of the day called for. While development was slow at first—just a handful of routes filled an early local guidebook—local climbers kept discovering new faces to climb, and the area grew slowly but steadily. Early route developers consisted of Tim Kosderka, Harold Hall, Tim Hart, Rick Brittsan, and Wayne Burns, and many of these climbers are still developing routes in the area to this day.

In the mid-1990s, Greg Orton, David Tvedt, Dee Tvedt, and veteran Callahans climber Harold Hall picked up the pace of route development, putting scores of new climbs up, both traditional and sport. The nature of the Tyee sandstone indigenous to this area is highly conducive to bolted sport climbs on vertical, overhung, and slab faces alike. By the year 2000, there were seven established areas at the Callahans, with more than 120 routes, some multipitch. In 2006,

Anna Eichner tops out the Mind Planet formation amidst a sea of clouds.

scores of new routes have since been established on preexisting crags as well as on new rocks scattered throughout the woods in this virtual endless sea of sandstone.

The Tvedt family and the Orton family are still quite active in route development and trail maintenance in the area. Greg Orton's website (*www.climbsworegon.com*) provides a wealth of information about the Callahans, as this is his home crag. Be sure to obey all closures posted on the website and by the upper and lower access gates to maintain access to this truly amazing area.

THE CALLAHANS BETA

Drive from Portland	▲	31/2 hours
Drive from Eugene	▲	13/4 hours
Drive from Bend	▲	4–4 1/2 hours
Drive from Pendleton	▲	61/2–7 hours
Approach times	▲	10 minutes to 1 hour

Getting there: From I-5 near Roseburg take the Garden Valley Boulevard exit (exit 125). Drive west, away from Roseburg, for 2 miles. Turn left on Melrose Road and reset your odometer. Then pick either the upper approach (Reston Ridge Road) or the lower approach (Touchstone Road), described prior to the trail approaches.

Time to go: While the weather can be wet in winter, the elevation oftentimes puts the higher rock formations above the fog in the valley below. 60-degree days in December are not unheard of. Roseburg gets hot in the summer, but again, the elevation can work to a climber's advantage, especially if you stay in the shade. The best time to climb here is fall through early summer, but climbing can be had year-round.

Rules: Access to the Callahans is on private land owned by Weyerhaeuser. Be respectful to ensure future climbing access to this area. Give logging trucks right of way on all roads. Do not block any gates, and allow enough room for other vehicles to turn around. Obey restrictions such as no vehicle access, no camping, and other seasonal closures for raptor nesting or fire restrictions during certain times of the year. For more information on closures visit Greg Orton's website, *www.climbsworegon.com*.

Camping: There is no camping close to the Callahans. See the Umpqua National Forest chapter for camping near the Honeycombs.

Food: The town of Melrose has basic amenities, and the town of Roseburg has a wide range of restaurants and grocery stores.

Climbing type: Trad and sport climbing on slab, vertical, and over-hanging featured, pocketed rock faces. While there are several multipitch climbs as well, all climbs in this guidebook are single-pitch sport climbs.

Rock type: Tyee sandstone

Gear: 15–20 quickdraws of varied lengths, extra locking carabiners, trad rack to 4 inches with doubles of midsize gear, webbing and runners of various lengths, 60-meter rope (2 ropes for some rappels).

Emergency services: Dial 911.

Nearest hospital: Mercy Medical Center, 2700 Stewart Parkway, Roseburg, (541) 673-0611.

Pay phone: Melrose Country Store.

Extras: Both kids and dogs are allowed at the Callahans, but it is not the most ideal site for either. As this is private land, dogs must be on a leash. There is no water source available on-site, so be sure to bring extra. The climbers trails are steep, and there is potential for rockfall, so be careful.

Other local activities: Paddling, fly fishing, cycling, mountaineering, and hiking (the Pacific Crest Trail is nearby).

Getting there from Melrose:

Upper approach driving directions (Reston Ridge Road): From Melrose Road, turn right on Doerner Road at 4.4 miles. Continue west on Doerner Road for 2.1 miles, where the road forks. Veer right onto Callahan Road. This road is steep and has a few sharp switchbacks. Be sure to give logging trucks the right of way, as they need more room to make these tight turns. Follow this road for 3.75 miles until the pavement ends. Continue on gravel for 0.35 mile to a gate (the upper gate).

Weyerhaeuser owns the rights to this upper Ridge Road approach. The company allows climbers to access the cliffs via this road, but this access is a privilege, not a right. Be respectful of this area. While this upper gate is sometimes open, it is often closed. This area is also patrolled by a security guard, so obey seasonal closures and fire restrictions to avoid future access issues. Even if the gate is open, it is recommended that you park outside of it and hike or bicycle in, as it can close at any time without notice. Be sure not to block the gate, and leave plenty of room for logging trucks to get through. If you choose to drive in, be sure to pay attention to signs indicating workers ahead or logging in progress. If you see these signs on the roadway, turn around and use the lower Touchstone Road approach, as logging can be dangerous, and the workers do not want to be disturbed.

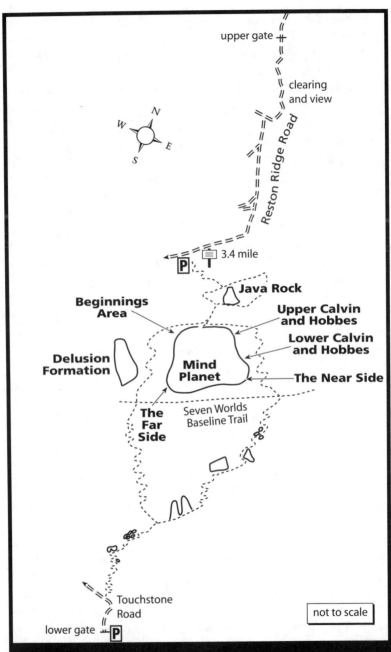

upper gate

clearing
and view

Reston Ridge Road

N
W   E
S

P 📋 3.4 mile

Java Rock

**Beginnings
Area**

**Upper Calvin
and Hobbes**

**Lower Calvin
and Hobbes**

**Delusion
Formation**

**Mind
Planet**

The Near Side

**The
Far
Side**

Seven Worlds
Baseline Trail

Touchstone
Road

lower gate P

not to scale

THE CALLAHANS

This upper approach can be confusing the first few times you navigate it, as you cannot see the rocks beneath you for reference. The best way to acquaint yourself with it is to either drive in the first time, when the gate is open, using an odometer to mark the distance. If the gate is locked, ride a bicycle with an odometer. If you follow the ridge road all the way down, taking the only major left you come to; it will lead to the lower gate along the lower Touchstone Road approach. Watch out for logging trucks, especially if the upper gate is open.

Reset your odometer at the upper gate, and drive past a large clearing with a view of the valley below to a left-hand turn at 0.9 mile. Continue past two right-hand forks at 1.4 miles and 2.6 miles to a parking area on the left at 3.25 miles. There is a sign at this pullout that says 3.4, which corresponds to a mileage chart from Greg Orton's 2001 *Rock Climbing Southwest Oregon* climbing guide.

Lower approach driving directions (Touchstone Road): Drive 5.1 miles on Melrose Road, then turn right onto Flournoy Valley Road (0.7 mile past Doerner Road) and drive 4.9 miles. Turn right on Touchstone Road and drive 1.8 miles to parking beside a locked gate (the lower gate). This gate is used frequently, so do not block it. Leave room for other vehicles to turn around as well.

Approaches: Upper approach (Reston Ridge Road): GPS reading at trailhead, N 43 deg. 13.234' W 123 deg. 33.994'. From the parking area to the left of the road, walk downhill on a trail with several switchbacks. Just after passing a boulder, veer left to Java Rock. Continue downhill to the right to access Mind Planet and the Delusion Formation. If the upper gate is open, this approach takes 10–20 minutes and is much shorter than the lower one. If the upper gate is not open, add 3.5 miles of road walking to your approach time. Note that parking outside the lower gate and hiking in is preferred by Weyerhaeuser.

Lower approach (Touchstone Road): GPS reading at the lower gate, N 43° 12.714' W 123° 33.780'. Walk past the gate 0.15 mile to the first sharp switchback to the left. Turn right on a small trail and walk up the steep trail with switchbacks for 0.6 mile to a fork in the trail. Veer right for easiest access to the Near Side and Calvin and Hobbes. Veer left for easiest access to the Far Side and the Beginnings Area. Both trails access the Seven Worlds Baseline Trail. Either way can be used for equidistant access to Java Rock. The approach takes 45 minutes to 1 hour. Follow specific trail directions to access the various areas.

While the Callahans is a large area with many different outcroppings of rock, the Inner World is one of the main sections with a wide variety of different climbs in a concentrated space. The shortest access to the Inner World is via the upper Reston Ridge Road approach, but the lower Touchstone Road trail leads directly to the bottom of Mind Planet. The three Inner World areas described here are Java Rock, Mind Planet, and the Delusion Formation.

Java Rock

This is the first rock that you pass on the descent trail from the Reston Ridge Road. These short, challenging routes can be led or easily set up on top rope.

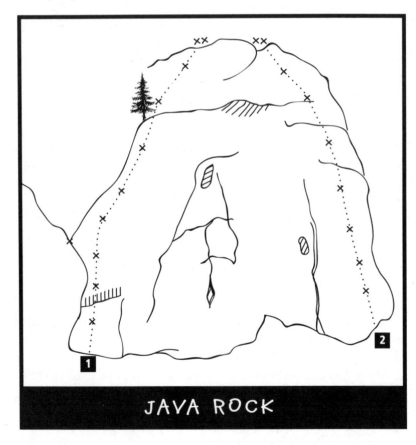

JAVA ROCK

1. BLACK COFFEE 5.9 SPORT ★★

FA: Larry Lynch 2000

This is the far-left route on the rock. Friction-climb the left corner up and right through slab face moves and a thin friction finish. 8 bolts.

2. ZOMBIE MAGIC 5.10b SPORT ★★

FA: Dee and David Tvedt 2000

This is the far-right bolted line on Java Rock. Climb the featured slab through a series of bulges and mantels. Finish left to chain anchors. 7 bolts.

Mind Planet

This is the largest rock at the Inner World, and it has a wide variety of routes. Upper Calvin and Hobbes, Lower Calvin and Hobbes, and the Near Side areas are on one side of the rock and the Far Side and the Beginnings Area are on the other. There is access to the top via a trail to set most climbs up on top rope.

UPPER CALVIN AND HOBBES

This is a good beginner area, with a variety of moderate slab climbs to lead and top-rope. Top rope access for the following climbs is via a slightly exposed ledge traverse. You can use the anchors from right to left as protection if you do not feel comfortable traversing unroped. Routes are listed from right to left, or uphill to downhill. These routes are often covered with moss or lichen, so a wire brush is recommended.

1. IT'S A MAGICAL WORLD 5.5 SPORT ★

FA: Keenan Tvedt 2000

This is the shorter route on the far-right, uphill side of the wall. Slab friction climbing to far-right anchors on the ledge. 9 bolts.

2. SPACE MAN SPIFF 5.6 SPORT ★

FA: Keenan Tvedt 2000

Face-climb the featured slab up and right of a slight bulge to chain anchors just left of *It's a Magical World*. 10 bolts.

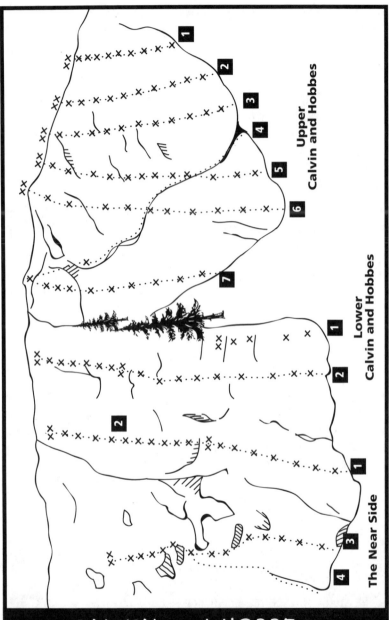

CALVIN and HOBBES
and THE NEAR SIDE

3. RED WAGON TO OBLIVION 5.7 SPORT ★★

FA: Keenan Tvedt 2000

Face-climb on the featured slab up and left of a slight bulge to the third set of chain anchors from the right. 11 bolts.

4. HOBBES TRAVERSE 5.1 SPORT

FA: David Tvedt 1996

This route is an excellent first lead, as it borders on fourth class. Climb up left in a shallow groove/gully on a solid 45-foot featured slab. Use bolts from routes 5 through 7 to protect your traverse, as well as a few extra bolts between climbs along the way. Shared single anchor with *Calvinball*. This route is often soloed, but one slip could lead to a major downhill tumble. Bolts.

5. STRIPES OF FURY 5.8 SPORT ★★

FA: Keenan Tvedt 2000

This route begins just left of *Hobbes Traverse*. Climb up and right past 3 bolts through the gully, then past 9 more bolts to the fourth set of chain anchors from the right. 12 bolts.

6. SUZIE'S REVENGE 5.9 SPORT ★

FA: Keenan Tvedt 2000

Climb the featured slab up and right past 5 bolts through the *Hobbes Traverse* gully. Continue past 4 more bolts through a slight bulge to the fifth set of chain anchors from the right on the ledge above. 10 bolts.

7. CALVINBALL 5.5 SPORT ★

FA: Unknown

Climb the far-left bolt line just right of a gully with several trees. Climb past 6 bolts to a dirty ledge stance, then up past 3 more bolts to a single anchor, shared with *Hobbes Traverse*. 9 bolts.

LOWER CALVIN AND HOBBES

1. THERE'S TREASURE EVERYWHERE 5.6 SPORT ★

FA: Keenan Tvedt 1997

This is a short slab friction climb just left of the gully with several trees. Easily set up on top rope. 4 bolts.

2. THE INDISPENSABLE ROUTE 5.8 SPORT ★★

FA: Keenan Tvedt 1997

Slab friction climbing. Note that there are two sets of anchors on this route: one about 70 feet up and a second set at the top of the route. You can set up a top rope by accessing the higher set of anchors from above via the Near Side ledge. A 60-meter rope is recommended. 15 bolts.

THE NEAR SIDE

These routes begin just left of the Lower Calvin and Hobbes routes above. All of these routes must be led.

1. THE DUCK POND 5.6 SPORT ★★

FA: Dee, Keenan, and David Tvedt 1999

Climb up the featured slab, moving right after the second bolt to a mantel crux at a ledge just beneath the chain anchors. 7 bolts.

2. THIN ICE 5.10a SPORT ★★

FA: Dee and David Tvedt 1999

This route begins above *The Duck Pond*. Climb the steep face through a small roof to finish on slab friction moves near the top of route. Chain anchors. 10 bolts.

3. ECLECTIC CLASSIC 5.10b/c SPORT ★★★

FA: David and Dee Tvedt 1999

Climb up the featured vertical face on edges and small huecos through one larger hueco to an overhung section in between two very large huecos. Continue on the slab to the anchors. 13 bolts.

4. RELATIVITY 5.10a/b SPORT ★★

FA: Dee Tvedt 2001

This route begins around the corner to the left of *Eclectic Classic*. Climb up the thin featured face to meet with *Eclectic Classic* at the two large huecos. Continue to same anchor as *Eclectic Classic*. Bolts.

BEGINNINGS AREA

This area is on the other side of the Mind Planet rock from Upper Calvin and Hobbes, Lower Calvin and Hobbes, and the Near Side. These routes are uphill from the Far Side. Routes are listed from left to right. Several short, easy top-rope routes are to the left and right of *Booder Skies*. All four routes below are easily set up on top rope from the access trail to the top of the rock.

Anna Eichner climbs the slab friction sandstone of Booder Skies.

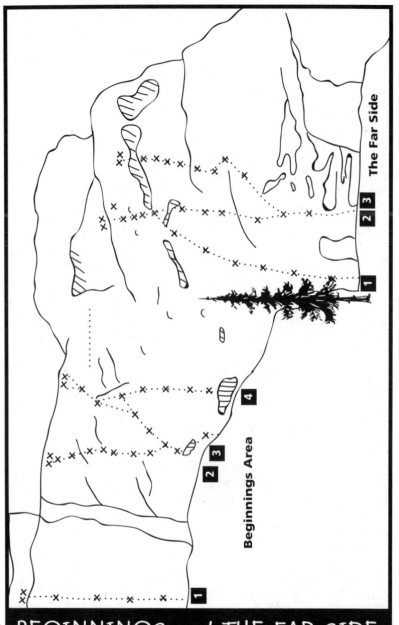

The Far Side

Beginnings Area

BEGINNINGS and THE FAR SIDE

1. A LITTLE FRICTION 5.7 SPORT ★

FA: Unknown

This is the first bolted line on the far, upper left side of the Beginnings Area, just left of a prominent dihedral gully. Climb friction moves over the smooth face to chain anchors. 4 bolts.

2. BOODER SKIES 5.6 SPORT ★★

FA: David, Dee, and Keenan Tvedt 1999

Start as for *All or Nothing*, moving left after the third bolt to a more featured slab face. Move up and left to chain anchors. You can top-rope a short 5.7 face climb to the left from the same anchor. 10 bolts.

3. ALL OR NOTHING 5.9 SPORT ★★

FA: David and Dee Tvedt 2000

Climb the slab face past a large hueco, moving right after the third bolt. Continue right over the blank slab face to meet up with *Balancing Act* at its fifth or sixth bolt. Same anchors as *Balancing Act*. 7–8 bolts.

4. BALANCING ACT 5.8 SPORT ★★

FA: David and Dee Tvedt 2000

Climb the featured slab face, smearing and edging to a ledge stance at chain anchors. 7 bolts.

THE FAR SIDE

This area is downhill about 10–15 yards toward the Seven Worlds Baseline Trail from the Beginnings Area. Routes on this wall are listed from left to right, or uphill to downhill. Routes get longer as you move down the hill.

1. ANIMALS WITH A LIFE 5.9 SPORT ★★★

FA: David Tvedt 1997

Climb over the slab with down-slanting shelves and edges through two large huecos to meet up with *Animals That Talk* just below a cave formation. Same anchors as *Animals That Talk*. 11 bolts.

2. ANIMALS THAT TALK 5.10a/b SPORT ★★★

FA, top rope: David Tvedt 1998

Climb past 3 bolts through a small roof bulge. Continue on a thin friction slab past 3 more bolts to the seventh bolt beneath a large cave formation. Finish through large huecos to chain anchors. 11 bolts.

3. ABSURD LIFE 5.10a SPORT ★★

FA: Dee and David Tvedt 2001

Start as for *Animals That Talk*. Climb the featured slab past 2 bolts, moving right of a small shelf roof through huecos and edges to the slab friction crux. Balance through the slab to larger holds, side pulls, and huecos to finish in the cave formation. Chain anchors. 10 bolts.

Chris Call belays Tim Dougherty on the Far Side of the Mind Planet.

Delusion Formation

This rock is just across the trail from the Far Side. The route below can be set up as a top rope with a short, exposed boulder problem on the back side of the rock.

1. MARTIANS AND TIN FOIL 5.10b SPORT ★★★

FA: David and Dee Tvedt 2001

Steep face climbing on side pulls, edges, and pockets to top chain anchors. 5 bolts.

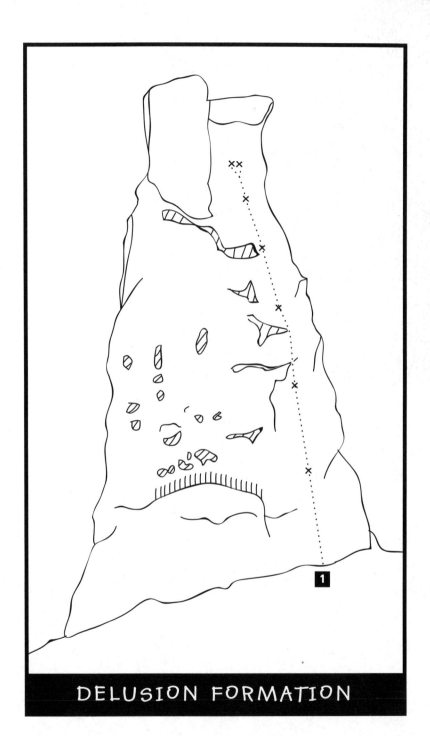

DELUSION FORMATION

Umpqua National Forest Area

Climbing in and around the Umpqua National Forest is abundant, but many of the areas either have few established routes over a large terrain or an abundance of harder routes. Both the Honeycombs and Acker Rock are crags with a multitude of beginner to intermediate routes, but they can be confusing to navigate at first. Be prepared to spend some time scouting trails and descents at these rocks before you dive into longer multipitch routes. Both of these areas also have seasonal raptor closures (see Umpqua Beta for details). While the Honeycombs has several top-roping options, Acker Rock is more for lead climbers, and most of the routes have multiple pitches. Be sure to come prepared with a honed sense of direction when you climb in this region.

The Honeycombs area is located on BLM land, just outside of Glide. It consists of three rock formations: North, West, and South Honeycombs. The West Honeycomb is closed to climbing indefinitely for raptor nesting, and the North Honeycomb only has a few established routes. The South Honeycomb is the main climbing area, and while it does not look that big upon first seeing it from the trail, this comb has a long ridge on the back side. The rock is volcanic in nature and resembles the welded tuff of

Chris Call contemplates his next move on Lower Fire Dome's unnamed 5.10b.

Smith Rock, although it is sharper. Faces range from slab to vertical to overhung, and the rock is highly textured with edges, huecos of all sizes, and broken crack systems, giving it a rippled, honeycomb appearance. Navigating this area can be confusing at first, and climbing here can be a challenge at times, as some bolt hangers are loose, some anchors need more webbing added, and some climbs have loose holds and runout bolts. While this area is only 10 miles from the nearest town, it seems more remote and has stunning views of the Umpqua hills and valleys. An elevation of over 2500 feet, tree-shaded cliffs, and hidden, cavernous passageways make the unexposed sections of the Honeycombs cool even in the heat of summer.

Acker Rock is located in the Tiller Ranger District of the Umpqua National Forest. It is closed for raptor nesting until roughly August 1 of each year, so the climbing season is limited. The best time to climb is August through November, before the weather makes navigating the Forest Service roads difficult. There is a lookout at the top of the rock formation that is accessible via the forest trail at the end of Forest Road 950. The Forest Service used to rent this tower out, but due to fire danger in past years, it is reserved for fire crews. There are several established routes at Acker Rock, with much room for future development. The majority of these routes are multipitch, and some can take the better part of a day to complete. Allow plenty of daylight when undertaking one of these longer endeavors. Also carry a headlamp and a variety of clothing in case the route takes longer than planned. There are three main rock outcroppings of varied heights, and routes range from 80 to over 1300 feet (when traversing the entire outcropping).

Overall, climbing in and around the Umpqua National Forest provides a sense of adventure. Whether negotiating the intricate passageways of the Honeycombs or tackling the state's longest traverse at Acker Rock, you will surely enjoy the backcountry feel to these established areas. Both areas were mainly developed by active southwestern Oregon climbers Harold Hall and Greg Orton from the late 1990s until the present day, although some routes were climbed prior to this boom of route development. For more information on these areas and other southwestern crags, refer to Greg Orton's series of southwest Oregon climbing guides, or visit his website (*www.climbsworegon.com*), where he updates raptor nesting closures and other local information. Both of these areas need some trail maintenance, and many of the climbs could use better rap anchors at the top instead of just bolts with webbing. Be sure to practice your knots, as some webbing may need replacing as it wears. Also, never rappel from just webbing with no rap rings or quicklinks. It is better to leave gear and live than to experience the alternative.

UMPQUA NATIONAL FOREST AREA BETA

Drive from Portland	▲	4–5 hours
Drive from Eugene	▲	2–3 hours
Drive from Bend	▲	31/2–4 hours
Drive from Pendleton	▲	7–8 hours
Approach times	▲	15 minutes to 11/2 hours

Getting there: The Honeycombs area is northeast of Roseburg, just east of Glide; Acker Rock is south of Roseburg, near Tiller. See each area for driving and trail approach directions.

Time to go: Late summer through early fall. Both of these areas are above 2500 feet in elevation, so the season is dependent on the snowpack for the year. Seasonal closures for raptor nesting also affect climbing. See the Rules, below.

Rules: The Honeycombs area is on BLM land and Acker Rock is in the Umpqua National Forest. Both areas have seasonal raptor closures that vary each year, but that generally last from January 1 to July 31. Be sure to follow the rules and closure regulations for each area. For the BLM, check *www.blm.gov/nhp/info/index.htm* or call the Roseburg District office at (541) 440-4930. For the Umpqua National Forest, check *www.fs.fed.us /r6/umpqua* or call the Tiller Ranger District at (541) 825-3201. Greg Orton also lists raptor closures on his website (*www.climbsworegon.com*).

Camping: For the Honeycombs, try the many designated camping areas along OR 138/N Umpqua Highway. For Acker Rock, there are several established campsites along Forest Road 28 within a 15- to 20-minute drive. See the national forest's website, listed above, for details.

Food: For the Honeycombs, Roseburg 27 miles to the west has full amenities, whereas Glide, 7 miles to the west, has only a gas station and several small dining establishments. For Acker Rock, the closest town is Tiller, roughly 25 miles southwest of Acker; Canyonville, which has basic food and amenities, is roughly 23 miles west of Tiller.

Climbing type: The Honeycombs has single-pitch sport routes on slab, vertical, and overhung rock with a multitude of pockets and features. Acker Rock has several single-pitch sport routes on slab, vertical, and over-hung rock over cracks, pockets, and edges. It also has multipitch routes with both bolts and gear placements. Be aware that these areas are more rustic than some of the more established destinations in this guidebook.

Rock type: Both areas are volcanic. Acker Rock is composed of dacite.

Gear: 15–20 quickdraws of varied lengths, extra locking carabiners, trad rack to 4 inches with doubles of popular sizes, webbing and runners of various lengths, 60-meter rope (2 ropes for some rappels). Bring a wrench along, as some anchors and bolts are already loose and others can become loose over time. Some anchors need readjusting at times, so be prepared with extra webbing and long runners. Many of the anchors consist of only 2 bolts and old webbing, making lowering or rappeling tricky without leaving gear, so it is a good idea to bring extra webbing, locking carabiners, quicklinks, or rap rings. Check all anchors and fixed protection before trusting them. Rappeling is suggested for most routes, to minimize impact on the anchors, as is leading the routes instead of top roping, for the same reason.

Emergency services: Dial 911.

Nearest hospital: Mercy Medical Center, 2700 Stewart Parkway, Roseburg, (541) 673-0611.

Pay phones: *The Honeycombs:* Idleyld Park Store, 2 miles west on OR 138. *Acker Rock:* On Forest Road 28 at the Bear Market in Jackson Creek, 5.2 miles off of OR 227. Calling cards, collect, and emergency only.

Extras: The Honeycombs area is dog- and kid-friendly for most climbs, although some higher ridge climbs are not ideal, as the terrain is exposed and littered with scree and loose rock. Follow BLM rules for pets. Acker Rock is not ideal for kids or dogs, as the trails are hard to navigate, slopes are filled with scree, and the area is less developed than some others in this guidebook, making it more of a backcountry experience. There is an abundance of wildlife in this area as well.

Other local activities: Mountain biking, hiking, fishing, paddling, and disc golfing.

The Honeycombs

Getting there: From I-5 in Roseburg, take the OR 138 exit (exit 24) toward City Center/Diamond Lake. At the end of the off-ramp, turn right onto W Harvard Avenue/OR 138 and follow OR 138 east for 0.6 mile. Turn left, staying on OR 138/N Umpqua Highway, and drive 23.5 miles through the town of Glide, past the Idleyld Park Store. Turn left onto

The South Comb of the Honeycombs

BLM Road 26-2-7, 1 mile past the Rock Creek Bridge and 0.5 mile past milepost 23, staying on the main road for 4.1 miles. At 4.1 miles, park on the right at a pullout, which is unmarked BLM Road 26-2-5.3. This road is blocked to vehicle traffic by a pile of rocks not visible from the parking pullout.

Approach: GPS reading at pullout, N 43° 19.912' W 122° 57.629'. Pullout elevation, 2624 feet. BLM Road 26-2-5.3 is blocked by a rock pile at the trailhead. Follow this trail 0.22 mile to an overlook. Veer right and descend roughly 0.07 mile to a major rock outcropping. This is the back side of the North Comb. Do not ascend this fourth-class trail, but instead turn left at this rock, scramble over some downed trees, and descend the steep trail past the base of the North Comb through chest-to-head-high manzanita bushes. This trail is aptly named Manzanita Ridge. After roughly 50 yards the South Comb will be in direct view downhill. Follow the trail 0.2 mile to a fork. Turn left and walk 0.03 mile to access the Fire Dome, the Secret Cleft, the Clock Tower, and Raptor Bluff. Veer right at the fork and hike 0.3 mile to access the West Corner. The approach takes 0.25–0.5 hour.

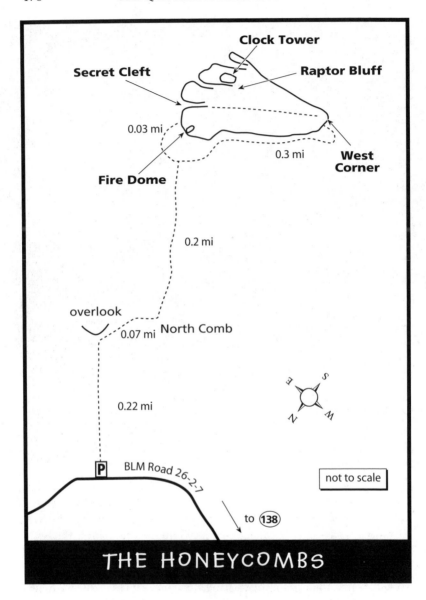

Clock Tower

Secret Cleft

Raptor Bluff

0.03 mi

Fire Dome

0.3 mi

West Corner

0.2 mi

overlook

0.07 mi   North Comb

0.22 mi

P   BLM Road 26-2-7

not to scale

to 138

THE HONEYCOMBS

FIRE DOME

At the fork in the Manzanita Ridge Trail, turn left and hike 0.03 mile to the base of the rock. The trail ends directly in between routes 1 and 2. Routes are on the lower level of Fire Dome and are listed from left to right.

Fire Dome as seen from the Manzanita Ridge Trail

1. UNNAMED. 5.9+ SPORT ★★★

FA: Harold Hall, Greg Orton

Just left of *Double Jointed*, this is currently the third bolted line to the right of the Secret Cleft passage to the top of the rock. Climb the featured face just right of a prominent overhang. The route moves through a series of overhangs on pockets and jugs. While bolts are well placed with good clip stances, some of the hangers are loose. Bring an adjustable wrench to tighten for safety. There is a 2-bolt belay with webbing and rap rings at the ledge just above a manzanita tree. Use long webbing for anchors to avoid rope drag. Recommended lead instead of top rope, due to drag. 10 bolts. Uses a full 60-meter rope.

Chris Call leading an unnamed 5.10b at Lower Fire Dome.

2. DOUBLE JOINTED 5.9 SPORT ★★

FA: Harold Hall, Greg Orton 1998

This highly enjoyable route climbs a featured face just right of route 1. Ascend a series of bulges up and right. The route moves just left of an obvious overhang to a belay stance on top of this ledge. There are 2-bolt anchors with webbing and no rap rings, so be prepared to leave carabiners or quicklinks. There is a second pitch to this climb, but it is dirty and not recommended. 6 bolts.

THE HONEYCOMBS
Fire Dome
(routes 1 and 2)

3. UNNAMED 5.7 SPORT ★★

FA: Harold Hall, Greg Orton

This route begins just right and around the corner from *Double Jointed*. Climb the featured face on pockets and edges past a yellow streak on the wall to a 2-bolt anchor with webbing and quicklinks. There is 1 bolt very low and left on the wall that protects the first thin moves. You can clip this, or simply skip it and stick-clip the second bolt. 8 bolts.

4. UNNAMED 5.10b SPORT ★★★

FA: Harold Hall, Greg Orton

Make a bouldery start on the overhanging arête. Climb through sharp pockets past 2 bolts to a vertical face just left of another arête. Continue up, using the right arête and featured face to a 2-bolt belay with webbing and no rap rings. 10 bolts.

THE HONEYCOMBS
Fire Dome
(routes 3 and 4)

SECRET CLEFT

From the lower level Fire Dome Wall, move left at to the first uphill passageway on the right. This is the Secret Cleft. Routes are listed from right to left, or downhill to uphill.

1. STAR GAZER 5.10b SPORT ★★
FA: Greg Orton, Harold Hall 1999
   This is the first route you come to on the right wall. Climb the overhang using small face holds and pockets. Bolted anchors. 6 bolts.

2. RABBIT HOLE 5.8 SPORT ★★★
FA: Greg Orton, Harold Hall 1999

This short climb is 20 feet uphill from *Star Gazer* on the same wall. Climb the overhang through huecos and ledges. Mantel the top to a bolted anchor. 3 bolts.

RAPTOR BLUFF
- -

About 15 feet past the Secret Cleft gully is a second and tighter, narrow gully that leads to the base of Raptor Bluff and the Clock Tower. You can also access these areas from a third gully about 20 yards farther down the base of the rock wall. This third-gully scramble is less steep, but it ends at a dirty 15-foot slab scramble over broken trees and moss to a scree trail beneath the Clock Tower. There is a way to access these areas by rappeling from the cliff above, but it is more confusing, especially the first time you explore the area.

Both the Raptor Bluff and Clock Tower routes have high first bolts, and although the climbing is relatively easy, a fall could lead to a major tumble for both the climber and belayer down a steep scree slope. It is recommended to anchor the belayer to a tree beneath the Clock Tower.

anchors not visible

THE HONEYCOMBS
Raptor Bluff

Nicholas Caselli moves past the first bolt while leading Breakfast O'
Champions. *(Note the optional natural pro placement in a pocket to the
lower right.)*

1. BREAKFAST O' CHAMPIONS 5.8 SPORT ★★
FA: Greg Orton, Harold Hall 1998

This climb begins on a runout, mossy slab to the first bolt. This section can be protected with gear to 3 inches in horizontal pockets. Climb
straight up the bolt line over the bulgy, pocketed face. The climbing
becomes slightly overhung at the top of the route. The anchors for this
climb are set back 3–4 feet on the top of the rock, so you will need long
runners or webbing to avoid rope drag. For this reason, the route works
better as a lead than a top rope. The last person to climb this route will
have to clean the gear from the top and walk off the rock through the
Secret Cleft. 4 bolts.

THE CLOCK TOWER

The Clock Tower is a free-standing pinnacle right beside Raptor Bluff, and it is accessed by the same trail.

THE CLOCK TOWER

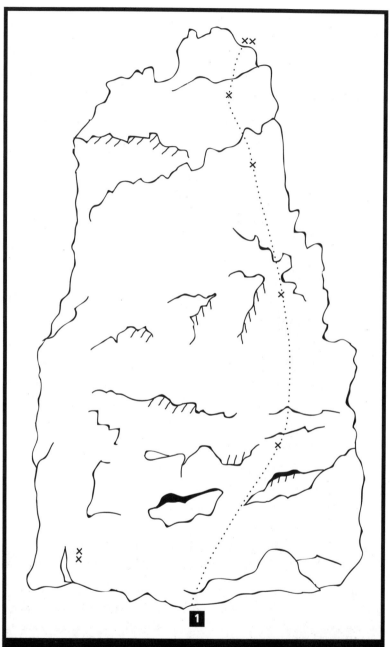

1

WEST CORNER

1. MILLENNIUM 5.7 SPORT ★

FA: Greg Orton, Harold Hall 1998

Starting from the small cavelike undercut at the base of the tower, climb up and right using the featured corner and a series of ledges. While sitting on top of this free-standing pinnacle is worth the effort, it is not a good beginner lead, as the route is runout and the rock is loose in sections. Although the actual climbing is only 40 feet, the steep hill leading to the base of the route makes the tower seem taller. Webbing anchors with rap rings. 3 bolts.

WEST CORNER

From the far-right corner of Fire Dome's lower level, pass the unnamed 5.10b overhanging arête route and continue walking a wide trail down a long corridor known as the Tube (due to the rounded overhang at the bottom of the wall here). Follow this feature for roughly 0.3 mile until the trail begins to veer right, away from the wall. Turn left on a worn path, scrambling up a small gully with a fallen tree to the base of the route.

1. STONESHIP 5.5 SPORT ★★★

FA: Tim Kosderka, Harold Hall 1978

The first bolt is 20 feet off of the belay ledge. Climb to the slight overhang, moving right and up through an abundance of large pockets, jugs, and edges, with beautiful views of the valley below. This route is runout, but there are a few pro placements up to 2 inches in horizontal cracks and pockets along the way. Watch for loose rock. Finish on bolted anchors at the top of the rock. Use long runners for top rope. 4 bolts. The best descent is to walk the exposed fourth-class ridgeline trail roughly 0.3 mile to exit right via the Secret Cleft.

Acker Rock

Getting there: From I-5 south of Roseburg, take exit 101 at Canyonville onto OR 227/Tiller-Trail Highway and drive east for 23 miles to the intersection of OR 227/County Road 1 and County Road 46. Turn left on County Road 46 just before the bridge and the Tiller Ranger Station. County Road 46 turns into Forest Road 28; follow it for 19.2 miles. Turn right on Buckeye Creek Road/Forest Road 29, following signs to Acker

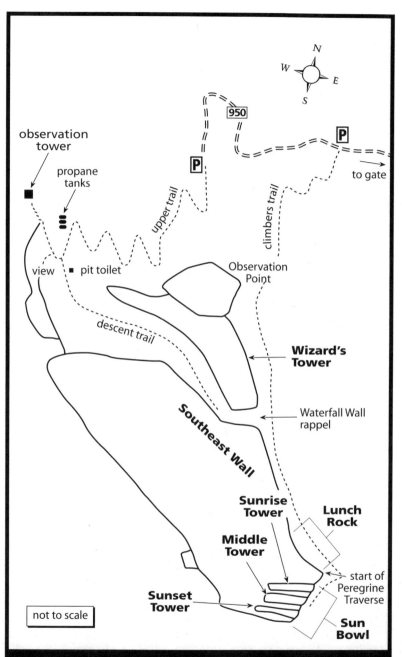

ACKER ROCK

Rock Lookout (the observation tower), and drive 5.8 miles. Turn left on Forest Road 2838, which becomes a gravel road for 1.5 miles.

Turn left on Forest Road 950 and drive 0.2 mile to a gate. If the gate is closed, park on the side of the road; do not block the gate.

If the gate is open, you can drive to the climbers trail approach or the upper trail approach. The climbers trail is 0.5 mile up Forest Road 950 on the left. It is a small trailhead, so pay close attention. As of winter 2005, the trail was flagged with light green tape. Refer to Greg Orton's website (*www.climbsworegon.com*) for updates. There is only a small pullout to the right for parking, so you may want to park at the lower gate and hike up, or continue up another 0.5 mile to the upper trail parking and hike downhill to the climbers trail. The upper trail parking is 1 mile past the gate; park when the road narrows and becomes impassable.

The approach takes 45 minutes to 1.5 hours, depending on gate closure.

Approaches: GPS reading at the intersection of Forest Roads 2838 and 950 (near the gate), N 43° 03.207' W 122° 37.879'.

Climbers trail **Approach:** GPS reading at trailhead, N 43° 03.302' W

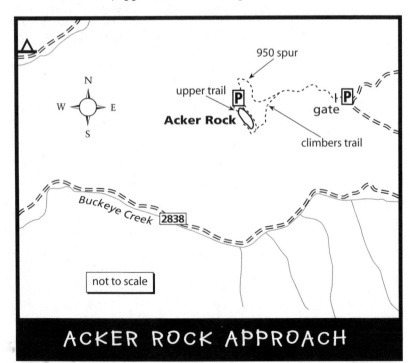

ACKER ROCK APPROACH

View from the Acker Rock observation tower (Photo by Radek Chalupa)

122° 38.518'. This trail is steep and hard to follow at times. Move over scree and loose gravel through previously burned forest. There is an abundance of rockfall potential, and the trail is littered with fallen trees. While it is only 0.6 mile from the trailhead to the Sun Bowl routes and the beginning of the Peregrine Traverse, allow 0.5–1 hour to negotiate this path, especially the first time you attempt it. Be sure to allow plenty of daylight to get out, as the trail is very rough and hard to follow.

Upper trail **Approach:** GPS reading at upper trail parking, N 43° 03.302' W 122° 38.806'. From the upper parking area, 1 mile past the gate, hike up the road until it narrows into a trail and begins to switchback at 0.15 mile. Continue uphill through a series of switchbacks, and at 0.4 mile, you will see propane tanks that supply the observation tower. The tower will also be in view at this point. At the next switchback there is a pit toilet with a beautiful view of the valley below. Continuing forward past the toilet leads to the descent trail through trees and scree toward the Waterfall Wall rappel. Continuing uphill from the toilet leads to the observation tower and the end of the *Peregrine Traverse*. You can get a great view of that route down to Lunch Rock by scrambling up a trail between the pit toilet and the tower, moving left along the ridge roughly 15 yards.

LUNCH ROCK

Lunch Rock is to the left side of Acker Rock, just before you reach the Sun Bowl, which is roughly 15 yards farther left around a corner. This area is named for the large, house-sized boulder that sits atop the cliffband, some four pitches up the *Peregrine Traverse*. This feature serves as a good natural landmark for routefinding.

The following route description of the *Peregrine Traverse* comes from Radek Chalupa and is reprinted here with his permission. He posted his ascent on Summitpost.org (*www.summitpost.org/show/mountain_link .pl/mountain_id/3760*).

Greg Orton originally described this route as twelve pitches in his 2001 *Rock Climbing Southwest Oregon* guidebook. The ten-pitch variation below provides a more efficient method of climbing Oregon's longest multipitch route.

1. PEREGRINE TRAVERSE 5.7 MIXED ★★★
FA: Harold Hall, Greg Orton 1999
The route traverses Acker's south ridge from its southern tip at the Sun Bowl area to just below the Acker Rock observation tower at the summit of the formation. With a couple exceptions, the route is a face climb—given the quality of the rock in Oregon, faces are typically cleaner and more solid than cracks or chimneys. Furthermore, the route is largely a sport climb—see the list of recommended gear and do not overexert yourself carrying in extra stuff. The route rating of 5.7 given by Greg Orton's guidebook seems quite soft. The pitch ratings and lengths given below are my own interpretation. Even though the route is ten pitches long, it goes by quickly, as the pitches are short and mostly bolted. All bolts encountered on-route look new and beefy. All belay stations (except for end of pitch 9 at the mouth of the chimney where there is a large tree for belaying) are nicely bolted with 2 new bolts each. Lastly, most of the time you are one or two rappels above the ground (rap east), making escape possible from many a belay station. These features make this route very beginner-friendly. A 5.6 leader will have fun on this one; a 5.7 leader looking for sustained climbing will be disappointed.

Radek Chalupa navigates the ridgeline on The Peregrine Traverse.
(Photo by Shirley Chalupa)

PEREGRINE TRAVERSE
(pitches 3—8)

summit formation;
route continues along ridge
not in view.

Shirley Chalupa leads her way up The Peregrine Traverse.
(Photo by Radek Chalupa)

Essential gear: 12–15 quickdraws, runners of various lengths, especially several long slings, and a 60-meter rope. While most of the route is bolted, also bring some essential trad gear. A conservative rack consists of a rack of nuts and one full range of camming units from ½ to 3 inches. A novice leader may want to bring more gear to practice placements or to protect runouts.

Pitch One: Fourth to low fifth class, 100 feet. Follow the low-angle ramp (or minor ridge protruding east from the main south ridge of Acker directly below Lunch Rock) up toward the tree where the ramp meets the east face of the main ridge. Belay either from the tree or look a bit higher and to the left for a pair of bolts. Bolts, optional pro to 1 inch. **Pitch Two:** 5.6, 60 feet. Climb 15 feet up the steepening face and traverse left about 40 feet, following nice bolts. You are traversing below a minor overhang. Belay from double bolts in a shallow depression in the face. Note that you could combine this pitch with the next one, but the rope drag might be bad. Bolts. **Pitch Three:** 5.6, 70 feet. Climb straight up a slabby face from the belay station. Look for a first bolt about 15 feet above the belay. Follow 2 or 3 more bolts to the crest of the ridge. Belay from double bolts at the crest. Bolts. **Pitch Four:** 5.7, 120 feet. Traverse fourth-class terrain 20 feet toward the base of a 30-foot, high-angle ramp (3 bolts visible from the belay). Move up the ramp/slab. This is probably the crux of the route, and it is also the most fun section of climbing. Continue up about 20 more feet of easy ground above the ramp. Traverse right following the base of Lunch Rock (about 30–40 feet below the top of Lunch Rock) over easy terrain (exposed third or fourth class). You will pass a small tree (optional belay bolts). Keep moving right for another 10–20 feet, where a pair of shiny belay bolts await you. Bolts. **Pitch Five:** 5.6, 120 feet. This pitch is easier to lead than it is to follow. Continue traversing right in the direction of the large notch in the ridge. Before the notch, move *up*, clipping a bolt, then look slightly higher up and right for 2 more bolts protecting the downclimb into the notch. Walk in the notch in the direction of the steep headwall in the ridge. Move up mossy, low-angle terrain on the left side of the crest and veer sharply right to a loose ramp to reach a nice ledge about a third of the way up the steep headwall. Belay from 2 bolts. Staying right of the ridge crest might be a better variation, but there are no bolts there and it looks harder (cleaner rock though). Bolts, pro to 2½ inches. **Pitch Six:** 5.6, 120 feet. From the belay, climb straight up steep rock with huge holds. Clip a bolt and continue moving up. The

Shirley Chalupa belays high on The Peregrine Traverse *with the valley unfolding below.* (Photo by Radek Chalupa)

angle quickly eases as you reach a double-bolted belay station near two small trees. Bolts, pro to 2 inches. **Pitch Seven:** 5.0, 100 feet. Follow the ridge crest about 40 feet, then move left of the crest where the terrain becomes steeper. Look for bolts. Belay on the left side of ridge crest from double bolts (located right of the next tree on the route). Bolts. **Pitch Eight:** 5.0, 120 feet. From belay, move up through a small notch. Follow the ridge crest to the false summit. This does not really seem to be the summit (the lookout structure seems to sit higher, actually), but this is where the register is. Belay from 2 bolts. Bolts. **Pitch Nine:** 5.0, 100 feet. From the summit, climb down the right side of the ridge (do not go too far right, just right of the bushes on the summit) and into the "jungle" below (about 50 feet below). Walk to the base of a dirty-looking chimney and belay from a large tree (slings) at its mouth. Bolts. **Pitch Ten:** 5.4, 100 feet. Move up the chimney (probably fourth to easy fifth class). Near the top, move right and up to the crest of the ridge. Walk the knife-edge ridge to its end (toward the lookout structure). Belay from one of two sets of nice bolts at the end of the ridge. From here, you will rappel 50 feet down on the right side of the ridge. At this point you are on second-class ground. You can store the rope for a while, but keep your harness on for the descent. Walk uphill through brush toward the lookout cabin, passing the pit toilet. Bolts, pro to 3½ inches. **Descent:** Like many multipitch or alpine routes, the descent is often the hardest part. If you do not need to return to the base of the route, simply hike down the Forest Service trail to Forest Road 950 and then down to the climbers trail or gate where your car is. If you wish to return to the base of the route, double-back to where the last rappel deposited you a few minutes earlier. Hike down the well-defined (forested and shady) gully between Acker Rock's south ridge (*Peregrine Traverse* on the right) and the Wizards Tower formation. As you exit the old-growth section of gully a few hundred feet below, traverse third-class slabs left (sandy, mossy, and generally slippery—be careful!) and make your way down to a "bowl" about 70 feet above the climbers trail (which you used earlier to access Sun Bowl and the start of the route). Do a single-rope rappel to the ground level. This is the *Waterfall Wall*, rated "mossy" 5.8, so rapping is a good idea for most people. You are now back on the climbers trail about 5 minutes away from start of route. Follow the trail (right if you are facing away from the wall, or left if you are facing the wall) to the start of the *Peregrine Traverse*.

SUN BOWL

Just left around the corner from the beginning of the *Peregrine Traverse* is the Sun Bowl. This wall gets sunlight for the better part of the day. There are three main towers on this wall that stand out from the larger rock formation about a third of the way to the top. From right to left, the towers are Sunrise Tower, Middle Tower, and Sunset Tower. The belay area for these routes is a sloping grass shelf that drops off drastically just before Sunset Tower. There is a 5.8 route on Sunset Tower, but the tenuous belay stance and potential for a large fall before clipping the first bolt make it dangerous to climb.

1. GOTHIC DOCTOR 5.7 SPORT ★★

FA: Greg Orton, Harold Hall 1998

This is the far-right route on the Sun Bowl, beginning on the right face beside Sunrise Tower and moving onto the main face at the third bolt. The first bolt is high; stick-clip recommended. Climb the featured face through pockets, edges, and broken cracks to chain anchors atop Sunrise Tower. 6 bolts.

2. SUNRISE TOWER 5.9 SPORT ★★

FA: Greg Orton, Harold Hall 1998

Climb thin face moves at the beginning through a series of bulges on the featured/pocketed face to the same anchors as *Gothic Doctor*. Sustained climbing on quality rock. 7 bolts.

3. WEENIE WITH A TAN 5.7 SPORT ★★

FA: Greg Orton, Harold Hall 1998

This route has two variations. Variation 1 accesses Sunrise Tower, and variation 2 accesses Middle Tower. **Variation 1:** ★ This variation feels more like a 5.8+, as it is accentuated by loose rock and rope drag. This variation is not recommended, although there are some exciting, overhung moves up high on the route. Climb to either the third or fourth bolt before traversing right. If you traverse up and right at the third bolt, there is a substantial runout, but if you traverse at the fourth bolt, there is a great deal of rope drag. Move up the featured slab through a dirty overhanging section to the same anchors as *Gothic Doctor*. 9 bolts. **Variation 2:** ★★ Move up the same featured face past 4 bolts, then

SUN BOWL

4 anchors
not visible

PEREGRINE
TRAVERSE

3

Sunrise
Tower

XX

Middle
Tower

XX

4

3

2

1

Peregrine Traverse
begins just around corner

traverse left onto a slab and into a dihedral. Follow the dihedral up, moving onto the right side of the Middle Tower face to chain anchors. The bolt placements on these anchors leave little room to thread the hanger and nut. They are often loose and need to be inspected each time you climb this route. It is a good idea to bring a wrench along to tighten these anchors down. 8 bolts.

4. STUDIO TAN 5.8 SPORT ★
FA: Greg Orton, Harold Hall 1998

Climb the face up to the second bolt, then move left over dirty, crumbling rock to a bulging slab face. Continue up the featured face on pockets and edges, through bulges to the top of Middle Tower. Shares anchors with *Weenie with a Tan*, variation 2. The anchors are often loose; see *Weenie with a Tan* description. 7 bolts.

Ashland

Ashland is a picturesque college town just north of the California border with three main climbing areas surrounding it. Emigrant Lake, Greensprings, and Pilot Rock all provide introductory level climbs as well as an abundance of intermediate and expert routes for climbers of all levels. The climbing consists of sandstone, basalt columns, and andesite respectively, with plenty of cracks, dihedrals, and featured face routes ranging from slab to vertical to overhanging. A weekend venture to the Ashland area will provide climbers with an abundance of quality routes located in the beautiful foothills some 10 to 30 minutes outside of the city.

The sandstone cliffs overlooking Emigrant Lake, a popular recreation area to the southeast of the city, were climbed for years before anyone thought to establish routes with bolts and anchors, so many first ascents went unrecorded. The main route developers for this area were Jerry Messinger and Jim Davis, and they began setting bolted lines in the late 1980s to early '90s. Climbers like Dan Higgins, Steve Johnson, and Nathan Kerr continued to develop routes at Emigrant Lake into the twenty-first century, and this area now has over twenty-five established routes ranging from 5.4 to hard 5.12. Chris Elder published an early guide to this area in the mid-1990s, entitled *A Climber's Guide to Emigrant Lake*

Chris Call tops out on the Poison Oak Wall above scenic Emigrant Lake.

and Greensprings. Emigrant Lake is a perfect spot to spend a day or two alternating sport climbing with sunbathing and swimming. The top of the cliffband also hosts a stunning view of Pilot Rock farther southeast.

The basalt columns of Greensprings are located within a mile or two of the Pacific Crest Trail along scenic OR 66, some 15 miles southeast of Ashland. Located on private land, these cliffs offer a fine array of face and crack climbs, both sport and trad, on just under vertical to vertical rock. This is the most popular local area, as most routes are easily top roped—although the scramble to the anchors can be tricky. Rock quality is good, and pro placements are relatively solid.

ASHLAND AREA BETA

Drive from Portland	▲	5–6 hours
Drive from Eugene	▲	3 1/2 hours
Drive from Bend	▲	4 1/2–5 hours
Drive from Pendleton	▲	8–8 1/2 hours
Approach times	▲	10–35 minutes

Getting there: All areas are southeast of Ashland, Emigrant Lake and Greensprings more east than south and Pilot Rock more south than east. See each area for driving and trail approach directions.

Time to go: Ashland can be very hot in the summertime, but many of these areas are at higher elevations with tree coverage. Emigrant Lake is at 2200 feet, so the season extends into early winter, but some of the rock is submerged under water during the spring and summer months depending on the amount of water released from the dam. Greensprings is at just over 4700 feet and Pilot Rock, located near the Mount Ashland Ski Area, has a summit of 5900 feet, so climbing is limited to late spring through early fall at both of these areas.

Rules: Emigrant Lake is a Jackson County park with an admission fee and rules posted at the day-use area. Greensprings is on private land, so respect the landowner's privacy, as he lives above the cliff. Pilot Rock is on BLM land, but you must cross several miles of private land to access it. Do not leave the roadway or trespass on private land to either side of the road. Pilot Rock is on BLM land. Follow BLM rules and be aware of seasonal closures. Contact the Medford main office at (541) 618-2200 for specific information.

Camping: Emigrant Lake has pay camping on site. Greensprings is close enough to Emigrant Lake to camp there. Not far from Pilot Rock are several Forest Service campsites, just past the Mount Ashland Ski Area, with suggested donations of $5 per night.

Food: Ashland has gas stations, grocery stores, and restaurants ranging from fast food to fine dining and everything in between.

Climbing type: Emigrant Lake consists of short, 25- to 50-foot sport routes on slab, vertical, and overhanging faces. Greensprings is a series of columns with trad, sport, and mixed climbs. Routes are cracks, dihedrals, and face climbs on slab, vertical, and slightly overhanging rock. The Pilot Rock route in this book is fourth class with the exception of a few short, exposed, easy fifth-class moves.

Rock type: Sandstone at Emigrant Lake; basalt at Greensprings; andesite at Pilot Rock.

Gear: 15–20 quickdraws of varied lengths, extra locking carabiners, trad rack to 4 inches with doubles of midsize gear (doubles of cams in midrange sizes for Greensprings), webbing and runners of various lengths, 60-meter rope (2 ropes for some rappels). Bring good approach shoes for fourth-class Pilot Rock.

Emergency services: Dial 911.

Nearest hospital: Ashland Community Hospital, 280 Maple Street, Ashland (541) 482-2441.

Pay phones: *Emigrant Lake:* On site just past the entrance gate. *Greensprings:* 2.6 miles past Tyler Creek Road, at the Greensprings Inn on the right. *Pilot Rock:* At the ski area when open, the first California exit (exit 790) at Hilt, or Ashland exit 13.

Extras: Several of these climbing areas are neither dog- or kid-friendly, as trails are loose with scree and rockfall. Emigrant Lake is a great area for kids, but pets are not allowed in the day-use area. Pets are allowed in the campground on a leash. Greensprings is on private land, so keep your pets quiet and under control. Also watch for rockfall from the cliffs above. At Pilot Rock, follow BLM rules for pets, and keep a close eye on children due to loose terrain and rockfall.

Other local activities: Paddling, fly fishing, cycling, mountaineering, hiking (the Pacific Crest Trail is nearby), and skiing/snowboarding.

Early to current route developers for Greensprings include Joe Chaves, Gavin Ferguson, Dan Higgins, Cory Jones, Jerry Messinger, and Don Ransom. Several guides have been written about this area over the years by Jerry Messinger, Mahlon Kerr-Valentic, and Chris Elder. Most recently, Greg Orton's *Rock Climbing Western Oregon Rogue* includes all three of the areas described in this section. Because this area is on private land, be courteous and respect the landowner's privacy; his house is just above the second, higher cliffband.

Pilot Rock is a stunning feature, visible from many viewpoints around the area. Although it is columnar like the Greensprings formation, it is andesite rather than basalt. There are roughly a half-dozen established routes at this area, but they are not recommended, as bolts are runout, gear is tenuous, and the quality of the rock makes climbing more dangerous than other areas in this guidebook. If you do choose to embark on another route at this area, be sure to have route information and always wear a helmet. The hike to the top of Pilot Rock offers breathtaking views of the foothills surrounding Ashland, the Cascade Range to the north, and Mount Shasta to the south.

The town of Ashland and its surrounding mountains and rivers provide a wonderful backdrop for a weekend climbing getaway. There is also some bouldering within the city limits, but due to the development of new houses in the area, access to these boulders may become an issue.

Emigrant Lake

Getting there: From I-5, take Ashland exit 14, heading east away from town on Greensprings Road/ OR 66. Follow signs to Emigrant Lake. Turn left into Emigrant Lake Park at 3 miles.

EMIGRANT LAKE
Overview

Poison Oak
Wall

Aqua Cave
Wall

Follow the road up past the earthen dam on the right to an entrance gate with a pay station. From the pay station drive past the day-use area on the right, campground on the left, and boat ramp on the right to a spillway on your right just before a bridge. Park in a gravel lot to your left, just before entering the RV camping area. Be sure to display your entrance ticket on the dashboard of your car or you will be fined.

You will see a prominent rock face up and left of this parking area. This is not the Emigrant Lake area; it is on private land. Continue walking up the road to the RV camping area to the very end of the campground. Just past the restrooms and showers you will see a gravel overflow parking lot with a gate, to the left of the RV campground beach. This is the trailhead to Poison Oak Wall and Aqua Wall.

Approach: GPS reading at trailhead gate, N 42° 09.595' W 122° 36.764'. Trailhead elevation, 2270 feet. From the gate at the overflow gravel parking lot, walk on a dirt service road following the shoreline for

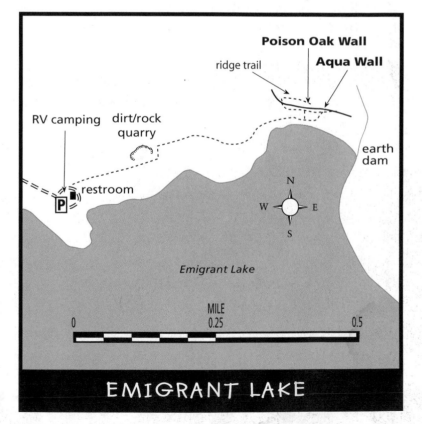

0.12 mile past a small dirt/rock quarry, turning left uphill on an obvious trail just a few yards before the road dead-ends into a dirty rock wall by the lake's edge. In the late fall, you may be able to scramble low around this wall, but it is fairly obvious where the road ends.

Walk uphill roughly 20 yards, turning right on the first trail you come to. Follow this trail 0.1 mile to a fork. Although you can see the rock to your left at this point, veer right slightly downhill toward the water. This trail will angle back uphill soon, forking left and right after another 0.06 mile. Turn left to reach Poison Oak Wall; turn right for Aqua Wall. The approach takes 10–20 minutes.

POISON OAK WALL

To set up top ropes on routes 1–7, follow the wall up and left past the routes into a shallow cave with a rock balanced over it. Just past this balanced rock is a short fourth-class scramble to the top of the wall. Routes are listed from left to right, with *Hippie Teacher* (route 1) beginning about 15 feet before you reach the cave.

EMIGRANT LAKE:
Poison Oak Wall

Chris Call palms the sandstone cliffs of Emigrant Lake's Poison Oak Wall.

1. HIPPIE TEACHER 5.5 SPORT
FA: Unknown

Climb the featured slab face through a series of horizontal cracks to a steeper finish. Carry long runners for one cold-shut anchor. Use the anchors on *Fire* as backup. 3 bolts.

2. FIRE 5.6 TRAD/TR
FA: Unknown

Climb the featured/pocketed face over horizontal cracks and ledges. Watch for loose rock. Pro to 2½ inches or top rope. Bring long runners for 2 cold-shut anchors on the top block.

3. MR. ANDERSON 5.7 SPORT ★

FA: Unknown

Face-climb through the left slot beside a 1-foot cap roof, using thin face holds and small finger pockets to reach the slab face, and then move over the large block at the top. Watch for loose rock. Bring long runners for the same 2 cold-shut anchors as *Fire*. 3 bolts.

4. BUG OFF 5.8 SPORT/MIXED ★★

FA: Jim Davis, Steve Johnson

Climb the featured face to the first bolt at a bulge. Climb the slab face to finish. Bring long runners for a tree belay. This route is a bit runout; use optional pro to 2 inches in the left crack. 3 bolts.

5. BEAVIS 5.7 SPORT ★

FA: Unknown

This route climbs face holds and ledges to meet up with *Butthead* at the third bolt. Bring long runners for the 2-bolt anchor on top of the rock. 5 bolts.

6. BUTTHEAD 5.9 SPORT ★★

FA: Jerry Messinger, Jim Davis

Climb through a series of ledges to a slight overhang at the second bolt. Continue on the featured slab face to a ledge finish. Shares same 2-bolt anchor as *Beavis*; bring long runners. 5 bolts.

7. CORNHOLIO 5.10a SPORT ★★

FA: Jerry Messinger, Jim Davis

Bouldery start. Climb through overhung blocks to a vertical face onto a block ledge. Finish on thin face holds to a horizontal crack and mantel top-out. Bring long runners for the 2-bolt anchor on top of the rock. 5 bolts.

8. REN 5.7 SPORT ★★★

FA: Jim Davis

Climb right up a ramp to the first bolt at a slight overhang, then move to a small sloped platform stance. Continue upward, right of a bush and through slab bulges with featured and pocketed faces to chain anchors. There are face-climb variations to the left and right. 4 bolts.

AQUA WALL

Veering right at the last fork in the trail, walk downhill, past *Ren* on Poison Oak Wall, to the next outcropping, which has a shallow cave in the bottom center. This wall is underwater for much of the spring and summer, but becomes climbable in the early fall when water levels drop. With a boat, you can climb it year-round.

1. AQUA MAN 5.10b SPORT ★★★

FA: Jim Davis

Start at the ramp to the right of the Aqua Cave feature. Move up left through a broken crack over a thin face to the first bolt. Negotiate the 6-inch cap roof, past anchors on the right, to the slab face and chain anchors. Moving right to the lower anchors will avoid the 5.10b crux; This 5.10a variation is called *Aqua Weenie*. 7 bolts.

Greensprings

Getting there: From I-5, take Ashland exit 14, heading east away from town on Greensprings Road/OR 66. After 14.35 miles, turn right on Tyler Creek Road, which is 0.8 mile past milepost 14 (the mileposts begin where OR 66 starts in Ashland, so miles are not measured from the interstate). If you reach milepost 15, or the Siskiyou summit, you have gone too far.

Reset your odometer and follow the road downhill, around a hairpin right turn at 0.5 mile, past a large gravel parking area on the left, to a parking pullout on the right at 0.85 mile.

The basalt columns of Greensprings

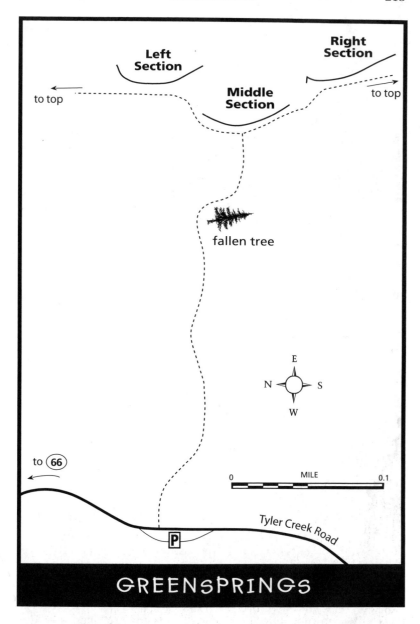

Left Section

Right Section

Middle Section

to top

to top

fallen tree

E

N — S

W

to (66)

MILE

0 ——————— 0.1

Tyler Creek Road

P

GREENSPRINGS

Approach: GPS reading at trailhead, N 42° 07.760' W 122° 29.505'. Trailhead elevation, 4711 feet. Directly across the road from the center of the parking pullout is an unmarked trailhead. Follow this trail up through a small clearing and then a steep uphill section for 0.25 mile to the base

Chris Call leads the Greensprings' classic Marge's Navel.

of the rock. The first wall you reach is the Middle Section, which is less developed than the rest of the crag. Turn left to reach the Left Section, and turn right to reach the Right Section. All climbs are listed from left to right. The trails at the base of the rock and above the climbs are not as well maintained as the trail to the rock.

There is an access trail to the top of the cliff via a trail to the left of *Marge's Navel,* but it is filled with loose rock and debris, so it can be confusing to navigate. Follow the trail for about 20–30 yards before it angles up and back right to the ledge above the routes. Be certain not to climb too high above the lower cliffband, as the terrain gets looser the higher you go. Many people choose to scramble up the fourth-class rock around the corner and 15–20 feet left of *Marge's Navel,* but this ascent is loose and dirty as well. There is also an access trail for the Right Section, just right of the cliff, but it is also relatively loose. The approach takes 15–25 minutes.

Although this is a popular top-roping area and some of the climbs below are recommended as top ropes, consider leading most of these climbs rather than scrambling above to set top ropes. There is an abundance of loose rock and debris above, and traffic at the top of the cliff is heavy at times. Helmets are recommended for belayers and climbers alike. Also remember that this is private land, and the landowner lives at the top of the cliffband. Be respectful and do not venture above the top anchors, and, while on top of the cliff, limit conversations to belay instructions only. Ratings at this area are generally harder than those at Emigrant Lake.

LEFT SECTION

1. MARGE'S NAVEL 5.8 SPORT ★★★

FA: Unknown

This route is located on the bottom of the most prominent feature at Greensprings, a free-standing pinnacle to the far left of the rock named

GREENSPRINGS
Left Section
(routes 1 and 2)

Stevo Thompson top-ropes Deep Purple's *crack.*

after the popular cartoon mother on *The Simpsons.* Climb the vertical to slightly overhung face over a series of edges and ledges past the navel hueco feature just above the fifth bolt to a slab finish at chain anchors. 5 bolts.

2. MARGE SIMPSON'S BACKSIDE 5.6 MIXED ★★
FA: Gavin Ferguson

Follow the slab ramp right of *Marge's Navel* into a stemming channel with cracks on both sides. Use both cracks and face holds, stemming up and right to a pillar ledge. Clip 1 bolt, then move left using face holds and stemming on the left pillar to chain anchors. Watch for loose rock on the route, especially up top. Hard for the rating; this is not a recommended beginner lead. One bolt and pro to 3 inches.

3. SKY PATROL 5.10a TR ★★★
FA: Unknown

This route begins just left of a large detached slab block. Follow the crack up to a flaring finger crack up top. While this route can be led with pro to 1 inch, it is more popular as a top-rope problem. Chain anchors.

4. DEEP PURPLE 5.9 TRAD ★
FA: Unknown

Climb the prominent crack up and right to chain anchors at the top. Pro to 4 inches, with doubles of midrange cams.

5. SKI TRACKS 5.10a/b TR
FA: Unknown

This is a prominent dual crack system with a flare at the bottom.

GREENSPRINGS
Left Section
(routes 3–5)

Climb using both cracks, face edges, and pockets. The route can be led but is difficult to protect. Recommended top rope. Shares anchors with *Deep Purple*.

GREENSPRINGS
Left Section
(route 6)

6. OFF-WIDTH 5.8 TRAD ★★

FA: Unknown

This prominent off-width crack at the far-right side of the Left Section angles up and left, just right of a bolt line for a 5.11c. While this crack can be lead with natural protection, some people clip the bolts to the left and treat it as a sport or mixed lead, finishing at the lower anchors to the right of the crack. This route can also be set up as a top rope, but be careful because access to the top anchors is via a fifth-class downclimb over loose, dirty rock. Chain anchors. Pro to 4½ inches.

RIGHT SECTION

Chris Call jams and smears on the strenuous Blitzfart *crack.*

1. BLITZFART 5.9 TRAD ★★

FA: Unknown

Climb the bulging crack to a ledge atop a broken pillar, just above an overhang. From the ledge, climb a thin finger crack to a slab with face holds on the right. This route is often dirty. Watch rope drag if top roping, as the rope is prone to sticking in the crack up top. Chain anchors. Pro to 2 inches; you may want doubles of midsize gear; save smaller gear for up top.

2. RAZOR CRACK 5.7+ TRAD ★★★

FA: Unknown

Follow two cracks up, using liebacks and face holds for stemming. Sustained climbing on holds that are often dirty. This is not a beginner lead. Shares chain anchors with *Blitzfart*. Pro to 4 inches.

GREENSPRINGS
Right Section

Pilot Rock

Getting there: From I-5 near Ashland, take exit 6 and follow Old Siskiyou Highway/OR 99 south for 1.9 miles (1.25 miles past the Mount Ashland turnoff). Turn left on Pilot Rock Road (40-2E-33) and reset your odometer. This is a private road for the first 2 miles, so do not leave the road or you will jeopardize access by trespassing on private land. This is an unimproved road, so four-wheel-drive is recommended.

Veer left, staying on the main road at 0.1 mile. Then veer right, staying on main road at 0.25 mile. A cattle guard at 1.9 miles marks the end of private land. Go straight on the main road at 2.1 miles. Stay right on main road at 2.65 miles. The road dead ends at 2.9 miles at an earthen road block. Park here, but allow room for other cars to turn around.

Approach: GPS reading at trailhead, N 42° 01.835' W 122° 34.208'. Trailhead elevation, 5103 feet. The trailhead is to the left of the earthen road block. Follow the trail for 0.25 mile to where it intersects with the Pacific Crest Trail on the left. Continue right, uphill, on a 6-foot wide steep trail for 0.4 more mile to the base of the cliff. The trail gets steeper and looser the closer you get to the rock. The approach takes 20–35 minutes.

Pilot Rock looms in the distance over picturesque Emigrant Lake.

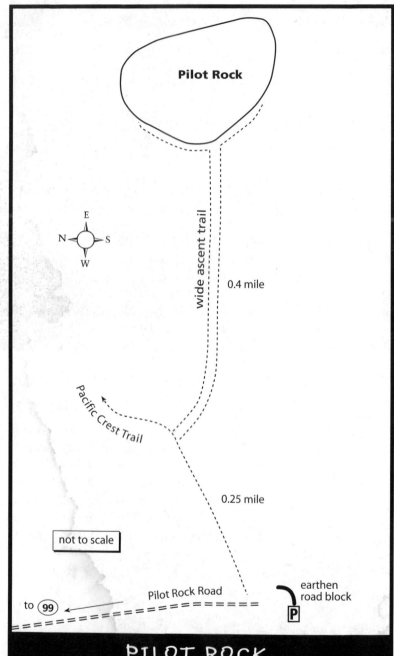

Pilot Rock

wide ascent trail

0.4 mile

Pacific Crest Trail

0.25 mile

not to scale

N · E · S · W

to 99

Pilot Rock Road

earthen road block

P

PILOT ROCK

PILOT ROCK

4th Class

1

1. MOUNTAINEER'S ROUTE (WEST GULLY) FOURTH CLASS ★★★

FA: Unknown

From the base of the rock, follow the rock left to a large gully filled with scree and rockfall. Scramble up this low-angle gully, moving left and then right up a steeper slope at the prominent tree. Just past the tree, move straight up through loose rock in a gully. There are several small boulder moves in this section that are a bit challenging, especially when downclimbing. This route is climbed without protection and is basically a steep hike with some exposed scrambling. Do not climb this route when the rock is wet, or if rain looks probable. Descend the way you came.

Eastern Oregon

Eastern Oregon has a variety of climbing types, but most areas are spread out over a wide distance. Much of the climbing that has been developed in this relatively mysterious part of the state is either far in the backcountry, with long approaches for few routes, or to reach a summit. While this climbing is highly recommended for more advanced climbers and adventurous mountaineers, it is not within the scope of this guidebook. Instead, this chapter contains a wide range of moderate climbs from two areas in eastern Oregon located near La Grande and Baker City. While these areas are not as close to one another as are most areas in other chapters of this book, distance becomes relative in this wide-open, less explored side of the state.

High Valley is a local climbing area, roughly 30 minutes southeast of La Grande, which consists of a small band of basalt columns varying from 35 to 50 feet in height. This area is located on private property, and the parking is limited, just off a gravel road with heavy local traffic. Be sure you don't block the roadway. There are several climbs located just by the bridge beside the road, but the majority of routes are on the other side of the street, several hundred feet up the hillside, within clear view and easy walking distance. Most climbs can be easily top roped, although some require natural anchors or directionals.

The French Gulch Spire's South Face at Burnt River

This area was mainly considered a locals' crag by La Grande, Baker City, and Pendleton climbers. It saw a surge of trad route development in the late 1970s and early '80s by climbers such as Lin Casciato, Mark Kerns, Richard Wilkins, Allen Sanderson, and Jim Brown. High Valley saw another boom in route development in the late 1980s and early '90s, with more bolted lines going up. Climbers such as Steve Brown, Elmo Hendrickson, Mark Hauter, and Lance Daniels began establishing more challenging routes, both sport and traditional, during this era.

Many bolt hangers at High Valley are homemade and bolts are old and subpar compared to today's standards, so be sure to inspect anchors and bolts whenever you climb here. Bolt hangers have been removed and replaced over the past decade or so, and it is unclear whether this is due to theft or other circumstances.

There are currently some twenty routes at High Valley, with the majority of them ranging from 5.4 to 5.10. Due to the rock quality, the angular nature of cracks, and the suspect quality of bolts, it is recommended for beginners to top-rope these routes rather than lead them. For this reason, most traditional climbs are also listed as top ropes. This area does, however, serve as a great place to practice placing natural protection while climbing on top rope. While it is not recommended to take large groups here, due to parking and the fact that High Valley is on private land with climbers granted access by permission of the land owner, this is a good crag for honing climbing skills.

Burnt River, roughly 30 minutes southeast of Baker City, consists of a series of limestone crags ranging from 50 to several hundred feet in height. All routes in this book are bolted, single-pitch, sport climbs that must be led. While Burnt River is on BLM land, most of the property surrounding it is private, so be sure to pay attention to No Trespassing signs to ensure future access. This area is much more rugged than High Valley, and most of the routes are accessed via steep scree trails. It is also overrun with rattlesnakes, so be careful on approaches. This area was developed by local Baker City, La Grande, and Boise climbers; Sandy Epeldi maintains a website with information: *www.boiseclimbs.com*.

Most bolt hangers at Burnt River are homemade, and some of the rock is loose. Approaches can be grueling, and the heat is unbearable in the summertime. With these factors aside, the cliffs of Burnt River provide some of the best, if not the only, moderate limestone climbs in Oregon. There are an abundance of 5.10+–5.13 climbs at this area as well, and local route setters continue to put up high-quality routes on this unique limestone outcropping.

EASTERN OREGON BETA

Drive from Portland	▲	4 1/2–5 1/2 hours
Drive from Eugene	▲	6 1/2–7 hours
Drive from Bend	▲	5 1/2–6 hours
Drive from Pendleton	▲	1 1/2–2 1/2 hours
Approach times	▲	5–25 minutes

Getting there: High Valley is 30 minutes southeast of La Grande, and Burnt River is 30 minutes southeast of Baker City. See each area for driving and trail approach directions.

Time to go: Early fall through late spring, as summer can be unbearably hot in eastern Oregon. You can climb in the early morning or evening at High Valley in the summer if you dodge the sun.

Rules: High Valley is on private land owned by Keith Kearcher. He has a sign posted at the base of the Bridge Wall that says, "Rock climbing is at your own risk. Owner not responsible for injury, damage, theft, etc. Please pick up after yourself." Be sure to respect the owner's wishes and leave this area as you found it, if not cleaner. Burnt River is located on BLM land, but private land surrounds it. Be sure to pay attention to No Trespassing signs in order to ensure future access to this unique area.

Camping: There are several Forest Service campsites in the Baker City area. See the Wallowa-Whitman National Forest website (*www.fs .fed.us/r6/w-w*).

Food: The town of Union is closest to High Valley, and it has several small dining establishments and stores. La Grande is roughly 30 minutes away, and it has full amenities as well. The town of Durkee is closest to Burnt River, and it has one gas station. Baker City is roughly 30 minutes away, and it has full amenities.

Climbing type: High Valley is a short columnar formation that has both trad and sport single-pitch climbs. Routes are crack, dihedral, and face climbs on slab, vertical, and overhanging rock. Burnt River routes are all sport with featured face moves over slab, vertical, and overhanging rock.

Rock type: Basalt at High Valley; limestone at Burnt River.

Gear: 15–20 quickdraws of varied lengths, extra locking carabiners, trad rack to 4 inches, webbing and runners of various lengths (including extra webbing), 60-meter rope. Good approach shoes are recommended for fourth-class scramble trails. High Valley has shorter pitches, so you can get away with fewer runners and a 50-meter rope, but you still need extra gear and webbing for setting and equalizing anchors.

Emergency services: Dial 911.

Nearest hospitals: *High Valley:* Grande Ronde Hospital, 900 Sunset Drive, La Grande, (541) 963-8421. *Burnt River:* St. Elizabeth Hospital, 3325 Pocahontas Road, Baker City, (541) 523-6461.

Pay phones: *High Valley:* Ash Street Shell station in Union. *Burnt River:* Gas station in Durkee at exit 327.

Extras: While there are no restrictions on dogs at either of these areas, they are both located on steep cliffbands with scree trails in a region known for rattlesnakes. High Valley is a much shorter hike, with a relatively flat area beneath the cliffband. It is much more ideal for both children and dogs, but watch out for rockfall and snakes and keep pets under control at all times, as High Valley is on private land. With the exception of the lower French Gulch Slab at Burnt River, neither dogs nor children are recommended at this area. The approaches are too steep, and the terrain is too rocky and wooded for either.

Other local activities: Paddling, fly fishing, cycling, mountaineering, hiking, and backcountry skiing/snowboarding.

The basalt columns of High Valley

High Valley

Getting there: From I-84 near La Grande, take exit 265 toward Union and La Grande. Turn toward Union on OR 203 south and drive 10.8 miles. Turn left on Bryan Street/OR 237 to Cove and drive 0.25 mile. Bryan Street/OR 237 makes a sharp bend left, but stay straight on High Valley Road. The pavement ends at 3.9 miles. Cross a bridge at 4.1 miles. The rock face is at 4.55 miles, just before a second bridge.

There is room for one car to park on the right, and there is room for a few more cars across the bridge on the other side of the road. Be sure to turn around so that you are facing the flow of traffic, and park as close to the edge of the road as possible. Do not block traffic, as this could jeopardize access to this area.

Approach: GPS at pullout N 45° 12.576' W 117° 47.454'. Bridge Rock is just above the parking pullout before the bridge on the right. There are several sport routes on this wall, the far-left one a 5.9, but the rock is so crumbly that climbing is not recommended here. The access trail to

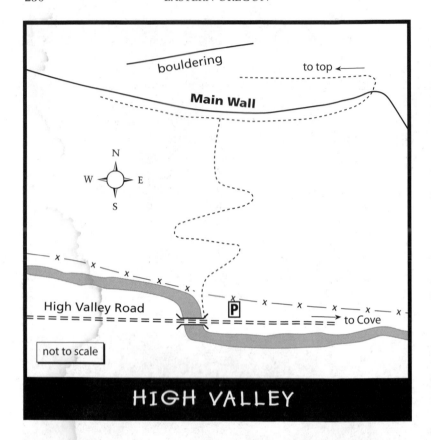

HIGH VALLEY

the main wall is on the other side of the road, where the bridge meets the barbed wire fence. Walk around the fence rather than climbing over it. This trail is short but steep, and it switchbacks up to the middle of the cliff. Be sure to stay on the main trail; do not take shortcuts to avoid switchbacks, as this will lead to increased erosion on the trail slope. The approach takes 5–10 minutes.

MAIN WALL

Routes begin just left of center on the main cliffband. Many of these routes are top ropes. You can reach the top of the cliffband by following the wall to the right and scrambling up a small trail between the main wall and the side wall to the right. There are also several boulder problems up top on a smaller cliffband. Routes are listed from left to right.

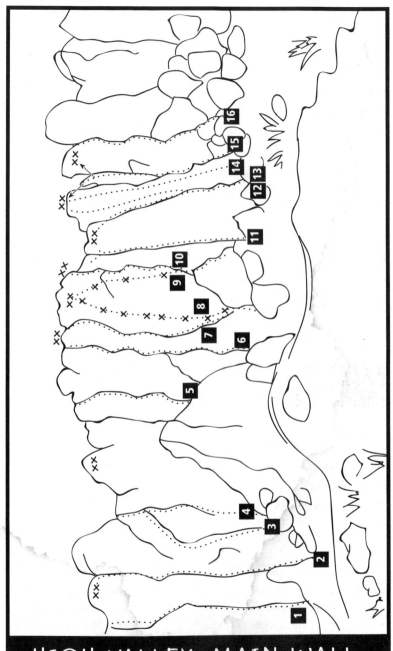

HIGH VALLEY: MAIN WALL

1. OLD BOLOGNA 5.5 TR ★

FA: Stu Ryman 1978

This is the far-left climb on the wall, although it actually lies close to the center of the rock formation. The climb starts in a crack system about 8 feet to the left of *Do or Fly*. Climb up the low-angle crack to a ledge stance beneath a wide slab crack to the top. No anchors; set natural pro.

2. DO OR FLY 5.9+ TRAD ★★★

FA: Lin Casciato 1977

This climb begins about 8 feet to the left of *Unnamed Symphony*, and it gets its name from the challenging off-width moves at the overhanging finish. Climb the short hand crack, jamming and liebacking to a slanted ledge stance just left of *Unnamed Symphony* and below a bulging fist crack. From here, climb straight up the fist crack with a couple of off-width moves at the top between two prominent bulging faces. The climbing here is solid 5.9+, but you can move right onto the face for easier 5.9 climbing on larger holds. Chain anchors on face to left. You may want to set a directional in the crack for top roping. This is a challenging intermediate lead; save large gear for the top. Pro to 4 inches.

3. UNNAMED SYMPHONY 5.9 TR ★

FFA: Allen Sanderson 1985

This climb begins in a thinner crack system about 6 feet to the left of *Last Hurrah*. Climb up and left through the thin crack to a ledge stance on an angled slab. Traverse right through a wider crack to finish on the same moves as *Last Hurrah*. No anchors; set natural pro.

4. LAST HURRAH 5.8+ TR ★

FFA: Allen Sanderson 1982

This route begins to the left of the prominent slab boulder that has vertical and horizontal cracks. Climb through a blocky vertical and horizontal crack to a prominent flaring hand crack in a corner. Continue to the top of the rock. No anchors; set natural pro.

5. AFTERNOON DELIGHT 5.7 TR ★

FA: Unknown

This climb starts on the right side of an upside down V slab ledge to the right of a prominent slab boulder that has broken vertical and horizontal cracks. Climb to stance atop the V slab, veering left to a hand crack left of *Pesky Rodent*. No anchors; set natural pro.

6. PESKY RODENT 5.7 TR ★

FA, tope rope: Stu Ryman 1978

This climb begins about 6 feet to the right of *Afternoon Delight*. Move up and left through a thin crack on a slab to a ledge stance beneath a hand crack. Continue up the crack, stemming on either face to the same top anchors as *Dusty Devil*. You may want to set a directional above crack.

7. DUSTY DEVIL 5.8 TR ★

FA: Unknown

This crack is just around the left corner from *Spacy Face*. Climb through a hand crack, stemming on the featured face to both sides. The crack widens toward the middle, passing a tree near the top. Use anchors to the left (same as for *Pesky Rodent*), setting a directional in the top of the crack, or place natural pro for anchors.

8. SPACY FACE 5.8- SPORT ★★

FFA: Jim Brown 1984

This route begins on a slightly overhung face to the left of a hand jam crack. Although the rock is loose toward the bottom, it gets more solid the higher you climb, leading to fun face moves on edges and pockets to chain anchors at the top of the face. Watch for missing bolt hangers. 8 bolts.

9. SAUSALITO 5.7+ SPORT ★

FFA: Allen Sanderson 1985

This climb begins around the corner from and to the right of *Spacy Face*, and it starts on a ledge about the height of the third bolt on *Spacy Face*. Climb past 2 bolts to a stance beneath a bulge. Move left, joining *Spacy Face* for easier moves, or climb straight over the bulge past 1 more bolt for more challenging (5.9) moves. Same chain anchors as *Spacy Face*. 3 bolts.

10. TRISH'S DILEMMA 5.5 TR ★★

FA: Lin Casciato, Mark Kerns, Richard Wilkins 1977

This crack is just right of *Sausalito* and just left of the *Classic Crack* open book. Climb the solid hand-to-finger crack, which splits into two cracks toward the top before becoming off-width at the end. Continue to a ledge, moving left to chain anchors on top of the rock, just right of the *Spacy Face/Sausalito* anchors. Be careful pulling your rope, as it could stick in the crack at the top.

11. CLASSIC CRACK 5.7 TR ★★

FA: Lin Casciato, Mark Kerns, Richard Wilkins 1977

This crack begins just right of *Trish's Dilemma* and goes from hand jams on a bulging face to slightly off-width in the middle, finishing in an open-book dihedral toward the top. You can move up and left to the *Trish's Dilemma* anchors, or use the lower anchors off right on the face that are for the 6-bolt 5.12 sport climb on that face.

12. SHIT EYE 5.6 TR ★★

FA: Unknown

This prominent crack begins around the corner from and to the right of *Classic Crack*. Move up through solid hand jams, veering left at the top. Use the lower anchors on the face to the left (that are for the 6-bolt 5.12 sport climb), or continue up right to anchors for *Fret Arête* and *Chimney Face Left*. You may want to set a directional above the crack if top roping.

13. FRET ARÊTE 5.9+ TR ★★

FA: Mark Hauter, Lance Daniels 1988

This prominent arête, just right of *Shit Eye*, is a recommended top rope, as the first bolt is high on the face. Begin climbing straight up the *Shit Eye* crack, moving left to the slab/vertical arête to reach the top chain anchors. Watch for missing bolt hangers.

14. CHIMNEY FACE LEFT 5.10b TR

FA: Steve Brown, Elmo Hendrickson 1989

This route climbs the face in between *Fret Arête* and *Smokestack*. Climb thin edges on vertical to slightly overhung rock, finishing at the *Fret Arête* anchors.

15. SMOKESTACK 5.4 TR

FA: Unknown

This route climbs dual cracks on a column to a ledge stance in a chimney. Continue up broken cracks to top anchors left or right. Watch for loose rock. You may want to set a directional in the crack.

16. TWO CHEEKS 5.6 TR

FA: Unknown

This route begins just right around the corner from the *Smokestack* chimney. Climb the broken blocky face to a wide crack system that flares in the middle of the route. Continue on easy ground to the top. No anchors; set natural pro.

Burnt River

Getting there: From I-84 in Durkee, take exit 237. From southbound, make a right on Vandecar and drive 0.4 mile; from northbound, make a left on Vandecar and drive 0.5 mile. Turn right on US 30 and drive 1.65 miles. Turn left on Burnt River Canyon Lane. At 1.8 miles, the pavement ends. At 9.1 miles, pass the Lost Dutchman Mining Association. At 12.5 miles, pass a small pullout and a trail. At 13.1 miles, turn right into a pullout just past a trail.

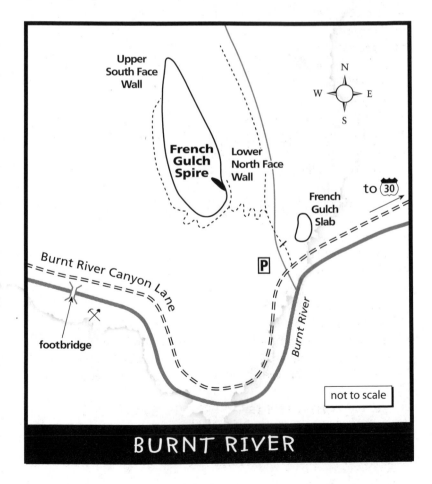

BURNT RIVER

Cave formation beside the 5.10b/c Lower North Face Wall

Approach: GPS reading at pullout, N 44° 32.799' W 117° 40.242'. From the pullout off of Burnt River Canyon Lane, French Gulch Spire is visible. Walk back out toward the road to meet the trail and then walk away from the river toward the spire. After 10 yards or so, you will come to a gate. Before you pass through the gate, you will see French Gulch Slab to your right. The other climbs are located through the gate up the trail. Be sure to close the gate behind you when you enter and exit French Gulch Trail. After passing through the gate, a short 0.2-mile hike will bring you to a creek crossing. Just after crossing French Gulch, turn left up a steep scree slope with several switchbacks. Follow trail directions for each area below. Approaches from the pullout take 5–25 minutes.

FRENCH GULCH SLAB

This wall is located directly on the right just before you pass through the gate. The routes are on the right-hand side of the rock. Unlike the other two areas, it is an easy approach from the car. Routes are listed from left to right.

1. UNNAMED 5.8 SPORT ★
FA: Unknown

Climb the featured slab past 2 bolts just left of a small ledge stance. Continue up between two small shrubs, using edges and side pulls past 6 more bolts to chain anchors just right of a prominent tree ledge. 8 bolts.

2. UNNAMED 5.10 SPORT ★
FA: Unknown

This climb begins about 8 feet to the right of route 1. It is a bit runout at the beginning, although the moves are relatively easy. Climb up to a solid ledge stance to clip the first bolt. Continue up the thin face past 4 more bolts, moving left to same anchors as route 1. 5 bolts.

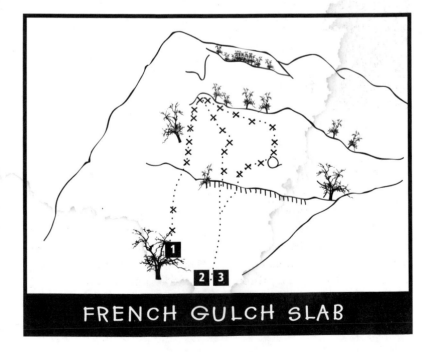

FRENCH GULCH SLAB

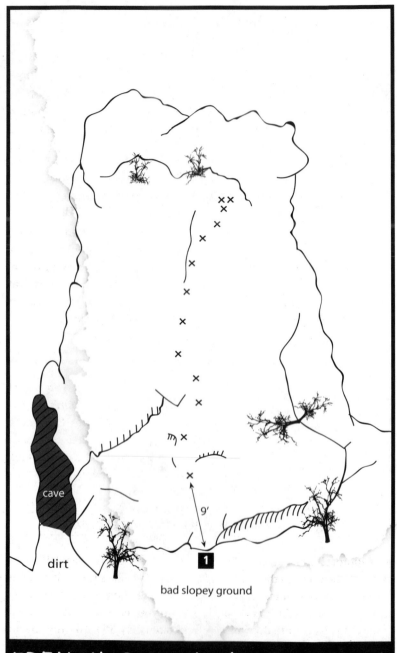

cave

dirt

9'

1

bad slopey ground

FRENCH GULCH SPIRE: NORTH

3. UNNAMED 5.9 SPORT ★

FA: Unknown

This climb has the same beginning as route 2 but moves right just below the tree ledge to clip a bolt, slightly lower and 8 feet to the right of the first bolt on route 2. Continue up past 2 more bolts to a prominent hueco-like feature in the rock. From here move straight up past 3 more bolts on edges and featured slab/vertical rock before moving back left past 3 more bolts to the same anchors as routes 1 and 2. You may want to leave some runners as directionals. 9 bolts.

FRENCH GULCH SPIRE: LOWER NORTH FACE WALL

From French Gulch Slab, continue up the trail roughly 0.2 mile, crossing over French Gulch to intersect with a small scree trail on the left just past the prominent French Gulch Spire. Scramble up the trail, staying on the right side of the spire for roughly 0.2 mile until you come to a rock wall directly in front of you with a large cave to the left of it. There is a tree and a boulder beside it about 5 yards beneath this rock face.

1. UNNAMED 5.10b/c SPORT ★★

FA: Unknown

This climb is well worth the short scramble up. Begin low on the face, roughly 10 feet to the right of the prominent cave. Climb the featured slab past 3 bolts, moving to the right of a small roof. From here, move straight up over a bulge to the vertical face on thin edges and pockets to the right of a thin crack. Continue upward, angling right after the ninth bolt to chain anchors on the face beneath a tree ledge. 11 bolts.

FRENCH GULCH SPIRE: UPPER SOUTH FACE WALL

The approach to this area is very rugged, to say the least. Veer left where the approach trail to the North Face/Lower Wall meets the rock, roughly 20 yards before you reach route 1 on that wall. From here, traverse left over loose rock, debris, and boulders until you reach a 50- to 60-degree scree gully. Negotiate this gully for approximately 50 yards, toward the top part of the south face. The routes will come into view as you ascend this tenuous trail. Begin moving right toward the cliff, meeting it just above a larger gully littered with tree fall and debris. Climbing this trail

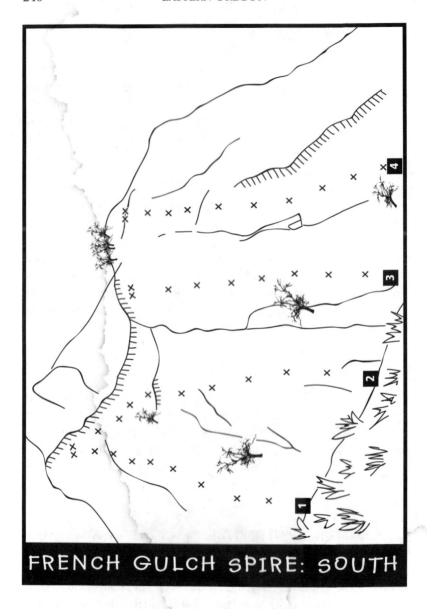

FRENCH GULCH SPIRE: SOUTH

is harder than some of the routes on this wall, but the ascent is worth it
for these four quality limestone lines. Climbs are listed from left to right,
or higher up on the wall to lower.

1. UNNAMED 5.7 SPORT ★

FA: Unknown

This climb begins highest on the hill beneath a prominent headwall high on the cliff. Since it begins farthest uphill, it is the shortest of the four routes on this wall. Begin climbing just left of a thin crack system on a featured slab past 2 bolts to the left of a shrub ledge. Continue up past 1 more bolt, crossing right over the crack past 4 more bolts to a left downward-sloping ledge. Step onto the ledge past 1 more bolt to chain anchors in a shallow dihedral. 8 bolts.

2. UNNAMED 5.10 SPORT ★

FA: Unknown

This climb begins downhill, roughly 12–15 feet below route 1 to the right of the crack and shrub ledge described above. Climb straight up the featured face to the left of a blocky gully past 3 bolts. Continue on thin face moves up and left past 2 more bolts, crossing over a small, blocky bulge. Continue left past 4 more bolts, moving just right of the left downward-sloping ledge to the same anchors as route 1. 9 bolts.

3. UNNAMED 5.8 SPORT ★

FA: Unknown

This climb begins roughly 10 feet to the right of and below route 2, just right of the blocky gully and just left of a small shrub low on the wall. Move straight up the wall through blocky broken thin cracks, staying just right of a prominent, small, right-facing corner, past a ledge at the sixth bolt to chain anchors beneath a tree ledge. 7 bolts.

4. UNNAMED 5.9 SPORT ★

FA: Unknown

This climb begins roughly 10 feet right and downhill from route 3, just right of the small shrub low on the wall. Climb just left of a prominent ledge ramp over the featured slab past 4 bolts to where the rock gets more vertical. Continue straight up past 1 more bolt, then begin angling slightly right past 2 more bolts to a small cap roof. Climb through the bulge and through 3 more bolts to chain anchors roughly 15 feet to the right of the route 3 anchors, beneath the same tree ledge and just left of a prominent corner. 9 bolts.

Appendixes

A. ROUTES BY DIFFICULTY

Fourth Class
Mountaineer's Route
  (West Gully)

5.1
Hobbes Traverse

5.3
Unnamed 5.3 (Salmon
  River Slab #5)

5.4
Smokestack
Smooth Operator

5.5
Calvinball
Hippie Teacher
It's A Magical World
Old Bologna
Stoneship
Trish's Dilemma

5.6
Booder Skies
Cinnamon Slab
Easy Reader
Fire
Giant's Staircase
  (Broughton's Bluff)
Giant's Staircase
  (Frenches Dome)
How Low Can You Go
Left Side Of The Beard
Marge Simpson's
  Backside
Moscow
Once Upon A Time
Plumber's Crack
Shit Eye
Space Man Spiff
Super Slab
The Duck Pond

There's Treasure
  Everywhere
Transportation Routes
Two Cheeks

5.7
Afternoon Delight
  (High Valley)
A Little Friction
Alpha Centauri
Bat Crack
Beavis
Bunny Face
Classic Crack (High
  Valley)
Dancer
Flakey Old Man
Fourth Column
Gothic Doctor
In Harm's Way
Leaning Uncertainty
Lichen It
Main Chimney
Millennium
Mr. Anderson
Nuke The Gay Whales
  For Jesus
Peregrine Traverse
Pesky Rodent
Purple Headed Warrior
Red Wagon To
  Oblivion
Ren
Right Side Of The
  Beard
Sanity Assassin Left
  Variation
Spiderman
The Lost Oxymoron

Unnamed 5.7 (Burnt
  River/ French Gulch
  Spire: Upper South
  Face Wall #1)
Unnamed 5.7
  (Honeycombs/ Fire
  Dome #3)
Unnamed 5.7 (Salmon
  River Slab #1)
Unnamed5.7 (Salmon
  River Slab #3)
Weenie With a Tan

5.7+
Acne Problem
Razor Crack
Sausalito

5.8
Ace
Afternoon Delight
  (Flagstone)
Balancing Act
Breakfast O'
  Champions
Bug Off
Dusty Devil
Edges and Ledges
Emerald City
Five Gallon Buckets
Ginger Snap
Hissing Llamas
Hop On Pop
Jeté
Lion's Jaw
Marge's Navel
New Chimney
Off-Width
Orient Express
Outer Column Jam

Out Of Harm's Way
Peanut Brittle
Pygmy Twilight
Rabbit Hole
Robotics
Rope De Dope Crack
Second Column
Spacy Face
Straw Man
Stripes Of Fury
Studio Tan
The Indispensable
  Route
Third Column/ Barn
  Door Lieback
Time To Shower
Tin Tangle
Toy Box
Unnamed 5.8 (Burnt
  River/ French Gulch
  Slab #1)
Unnamed 5.8 (Burnt
  River/ French Gulch
  Spire: Upper South
  Face Wall #3)
Unnamed 5.8 (Skinner
  Butte/ Wilderness
  Wall #2)

5.8+

Last Hurrah
New Generation
Scarface
The Hammer

5.9

All Or Nothing
Ancylostoma
Animals With A Life
Black Coffee
Blitzfart
Butthead
DaKind
Deep Pocket
Deep Purple
Do It Again

Double Jointed
Expresso
Forthright
Gandalf's Grip
  Variation
Grass Crack
Gunsmoke
Helium Woman
Moonshine Dihedral
Neptune
Nook And Cranny
Northern Lights
Outsiders
Phone Call From Satan
Revelations
Rubicon
Shamu
Silence Of The Cams
Snuffy Smith Buttress
Stained Glass
Streamline
Sunrise Tower
Suzie's Revenge
The Hydrotube
The Sickle
Traffic Court
Unnamed 5.9 (Burnt
  River/ French Gulch
  Slab #3)
Unnamed 5.9 (Burnt
  River/ French Gulch
  Spire: Upper South
  Face Wall #4)
Unnamed 5.9 (Salmon
  River Slab #2)
Unnamed 5.9 (Salmon
  River Slab #4)
Unnamed Symphony
Vertical Therapy

5.9+

Blueberry Jam
Classic Crack
Do Or Fly
Fret Arête

Gandalf's Grip
Jack Of Hearts
Light On The Path
Unnamed
  (Honeycombs/ Fire
  Dome #1)
Weird Lieback

5.10

Sanity Assassin Right
  Variation
Unnamed 5.10 (Burnt
  River/ French Gulch
  Slab #2)
Unnamed 5.10 (Burnt
  River/ French Gulch
  Spire: Upper South
  Face Wall #2)

5.10 a

Absurd Life
Captain Xenolith
Cornholio
Cosmos
Dances With Clams
Drill 'Em And Fill 'Em
Fifth Column/ Sign
  Face
Hard Lieback
Inversion Excursion
Irreverence
Morning Desire
Panes Of Reality
Phoenix
Pop Goes The Nubbin
Right Ski Track
Sheer Madness
Sky Patrol
Thin Ice

5.10 a/b

Animals That Talk
Clearasil
Jet Stream
Relativity
Ski Tracks

5.10 b

Aqua Man
Barbeque The Pope
Chimney Face Left
Float Like A Butterfly
Games Without
　Frontiers
JT's Route
Lake Of Fire
Let's Face It
Martians And Tin Foil
Nightingales On
　Vacation

Nine Gallon Buckets
Red Eye
Rites Of Passage
Screaming Yellow
　Zonkers
Silver Streak
Star Gazer
Unnamed
　(Honeycombs/ Fire
　Dome #4)
Wedding Day
Zombie Magic

5.10 b/c

Eclectic Classic
Gumby/ Morning Sky
Limpdick
Scene Of The Crime
Unnamed 5.10 b/c
　(Bulo Point)
Unnamed 5.10 b/c
　(Burnt River/ French
　Gulch Spire: Lower
　North Face Wall #1)

B. ROUTES BY RATING

★★★

Acne Problem 5.7+
Animals That Talk 5.10
　a/b
Animals With A Life
　5.9
Aqua Man 5.10 b
Barbeque The Pope
　5.10 b
Blueberry Jam 5.9+
Cinnamon Slab 5.6
Cosmos 5.10 a
DaKind 5.9
Dancer 5.7
Deep Pocket 5.9
Do Or Fly 5.9+
Eclectic Classic 5.10
　b/c
Five Gallon Buckets
　5.8
Games Without
　Frontiers 5.10 b
Gandalf's Grip 5.9+
Giant's Staircase
　(Frenches Dome) 5.6
Gumby/ Morning Sky
　5.10 b/c

Hop On Pop 5.8
Jet Stream 5.10 a/b
Light On The Path
　5.9+
Limpdick 5.10 b/c
Marge's Navel 5.8
Martians and Tin Foil
　5.10 b
Moonshine Dihedral
　5.9
Moscow 5.6
Mountaineer's Route
　(West Gully) 4th
　Class
Northern Lights 5.9
Peregrine Traverse 5.7
Phoenix 5.10 a
Rabbit Hole 5.8
Razor Crack 5.7+
Ren 5.7
Rubicon 5.9
Scene Of The Crime
　5.10 b/c
Screaming Yellow
　Zonkers 5.10 b
Silver Streak 5.10 b
Sky Patrol 5.10 a

Spiderman 5.7
Stoneship 5.5
Super Slab 5.6
The Hydrotube 5.8
Time To Shower 5.8
Traffic Court 5.9
Unnamed 5.10 b/c
　(Bulo Point/ First
　Main Face #2)
Unnamed 5.9+
　Honeycombs
Unnamed 5.10 b
　Honeycombs
Unnamed 5.9 (Salmon
　River Slab #2)

★★

Absurd Life 5.10 a
Ace 5.8
All Or Nothing 5.9
Alpha Centauri 5.7
Ancylostoma 5.9
Balancing Act 5.8
Black Coffee 5.9
Blitzfart 5.9
Booder Skies 5.6
Breakfast O'
　Champions 5.8

Bug Off 5.8

Bunny Face 5.7

Butthead 5.9

Captain Xenolith 5.10 a

Classic Crack (Broughton's Bluff) 5.9+

Classic Crack (High Valley) 5.7

Clearasil 5.10 a/b

Cornholio 5.10 a

Dances With Clams 5.10 a

Double Jointed 5.9

Drill 'Em And Fill 'Em 5.10 a

Easy Reader 5.6

Edges And Ledges 5.8

Emerald City 5.8

Expresso 5.9

Flakey Old Man 5.7

Float Like A Butterfly 5.10 b

Forthright 5.9

Fret Arête 5.9+

Gandalf's Grip Variation 5.9

Ginger Snap 5.8

Gothic Doctor 5.7

Hard Lieback 5.10 a

Helium Woman 5.9

Hissing Llamas 5.8

How Low Can You Go 5.6

In Harm's Way 5.7

Irreverence 5.10 a

Jack Of Hearts 5.9+

Jeté 5.8

JT's Route 5.10 b

Lake Of Fire 5.10 b

Leaning Uncertainty 5.7

Left Side Of The Beard 5.6

Let's Face It 5.10 b

Lichen It 5.7

Lion's Jaw 5.8

Marge Simpson's Backside 5.6

New Generation 5.8+

Nightingales On Vacation 5.10 b

Nine Gallon Buckets 5.10 b

Nuke The Gay Whales For Jesus 5.7

Off-Width 5.8

Once Upon A Time 5.6

Orient Express 5.8

Outer Column Jam 5.8

Out Of Harm's Way 5.8

Outsiders 5.9

Peanut Brittle 5.8

Phone Call From Satan 5.9

Pop Goes The Nubbin 5.10 a

Pygmy Twilight 5.8

Red Eye 5.10 b

Red Wagon To Oblivion 5.7

Relativity 5.10 a/b

Revelations 5.9

Right Side Of The Beard 5.7

Rites Of Passage 5.10 b

Robotics 5.8

Rope De Dope Crack 5.8

Scarface 5.8+

Shamu 5.9

Sheer Madness 5.10 a

Shit Eye 5.6

Silence Of The Cams 5.9

Snuffy Smith Buttress 5.9

Spacy Face 5.8

Star Gazer 5.10 b

Straw Man 5.8

Streamline 5.9

Stripes Of Fury 5.8

Sunrise Tower 5.9

The Duck Pond 5.6

The Hammer 5.8+

The Indispensable Route 5.8

The Lost Oxymoron 5.7

The Purple Headed Warrior 5.7

The Sickle 5.9

Thin Ice 5.10 a

Tin Tangle 5.8

Toy Box 5.8

Traffic Court 5.9

Trish's Dilemma 5.5

Unnamed 5.10 b/c (Burnt River/ French Gulch Spire: Lower North Face Wall #1)

Unnamed 5.7 (Honeycombs/ Lower Fire Dome #3)

Unnamed 5.7 (Salmon River Slab #1)

Unnamed 5.8 (Skinner Butte/ Wilderness Wall #2)

Vertical Therapy 5.9

Wedding Day 5.10 b

Weenie With A Tan Variation 2 5.7

Zombie Magic 5.10 b

★

Afternoon Delight 5.7 (High Valley)

Afternoon Delight 5.8 (Skinner Butte)

A Little Friction 5.7
Bat Crack 5.7
Beavis 5.7
Calvinball 5.5
Deep Purple 5.9
Do It Again 5.9
Dusty Devil 5.7
Fifth Column/ Sign
   Face 5.10 a
Fourth Column 5.7
Giant's Staircase
   (Broughton's Bluff)
   5.6
Grass Crack 5.9
Gunsmoke 5.9
Inversion Excursion
   5.10 a
It's A Magical World
   5.5
Last Hurrah 5.8
Main Chimney 5.7
Millennium 5.7
Mr. Anderson 5.7
New Chimney 5.8
Nook And Cranny 5.9
Old Bologna 5.5
Panes Of Reality 5.10 a
Pesky Rodent 5.7
Plumber's Crack 5.6
Right Ski Track 5.10 a
Sausalito 5.7+

Second Column 5.8
Smooth Operator 5.4
Spaceman Spiff 5.6
Stained Glass 5.9
Studio Tan 5.8
Suzie's Revenge 5.9
There's Treasure
   Everywhere 5.6
Third Column/ Barn
   Door Lieback 5.8
Unnamed 5.8 (Burnt
   River/ French Gulch
   Slab #1)
Unnamed 5.10 (Burnt
   River/ French Gulch
   Slab #2)
Unnamed 5.9 (Burnt
   River/ French Gulch
   Slab #3)
Unnamed 5.7 (Burnt
   River/ French Gulch
   Spire: Upper South
   Face Wall #1)
Unnamed 5.10 (Burnt
   River/ French Gulch
   Spire: Upper South
   Face Wall #2)
Unnamed 5.8 (Burnt
   River/ French Gulch
   Spire: Upper South
   Face Wall #3)

Unnamed 5.9 (Burnt
   River/ French Gulch
   Spire: Upper South
   Face Wall #4)
Unnamed 5.7 (Salmon
   River Slab #3)
Unnamed 5.9 (Salmon
   River Slab #4)
Unnamed Symphony
   5.9
Weenie With A Tan
   Variation 1 5.7
Weird Lieback 5.9+

No Stars

Chimney Face Left
   5.10 b
Fire 5.6
Hippie Teacher 5.5
Hobbes Traverse 5.0
Neptune 5.9
Ski Tracks 5.10 a/b
Smokestack 5.4
Transportation Routes
   5.6
Two Cheeks 5.6
Unnamed 5.3 (Salmon
   River Slab #5)

Bibliography

BOOKS

Bishop, Ellen Morris. *Hiking Oregon's Geology*. Seattle, WA: The Mountaineers Books, 2004.

Cossel, Don, and Dain Smoland. *Bulo Point Rock Climbs*. Self-published.

Dodge, Nicholas A. *A Climbing Guide to Oregon*. Beaverton, OR: The Touchstone Press, 1975.

Lawson, Ryan. *New Sh!tuff at Smith*. Self-published, 2001.

Olson, Tim. *Portland Rock Climbs: A Climber's Guide to Northwest Oregon*. Chelsea, MI: Sheridan Books, 2001.

Orton, Greg. *Rock Climbing Southwest Oregon*. La Crescenta, CA: Mountain N' Air Books, 2001.

———. *Rock Climbing Western Oregon Rogue*. La Crescenta, CA: Mountain N' Air Books, 2005.

———. *Rock Climbing Western Oregon Willamette*. La Crescenta, CA: Mountain N' Air Books, 2005.

Watts, Alan. *Climber's Guide to Smith Rock*. Evergreen, CO: Chockstone Press, 1992.

Whitelaw, David. *Weekend Rock Washington*. Seattle, WA: The Mountaineers Books, 2005.

PERIODICALS

"High Valley, Anthony Lakes Northeast Report." *Climbing Magazine*, no. 100 (February 1987), p. 14.

"New Routes." *Climbing Magazine*, no. 119 (September 1988), p. 228.

ABOUT THE UIAA/TABLE OF DIFFICULTIES

UIAA

The UIAA encourages the inclusion of information in guidebooks that helps visitors from overseas to understand the most important information about local access, grades and emergency procedures. The UIAA also encourages climbers and mountaineers to share knowledge and views on issues such as safety, ethics, and good practice in mountain sports. The UIAA is not responsible for, and accepts no liability for, the technical content or accuracy of the information in this guidebook. Climbing, hill walking, and mountaineering are activities with a danger of personal injury and death. Participants should be aware of, understand, and accept these risks and be responsible for their own actions and involvement.

INTERNATIONAL GRADE COMPARISON CHART

UIAA	USA	GB	F	D	AUS
V−	5.5	4a	5a	V	13
V	5.6	4b	5b	VI	14
V+	5.7	4c	5c	VI	14
VI−	5.8	4c	5c	VIIa	15
VI	5.9	5a	6a	VIIb	16
VI+	5.10a	5a	6a+	VIIc	16
VII−	5.10b	5b	6b	VIIIa	17
VII	5.10c	5b	6b+	VIIIb	18
VII+	5.10d	5c	6c	VIIIc	19
VIII−	5.11a	6a	6c+	IXa	20
VIII−	5.11b	6a	6c+	IXa	21
VIII	5.11c	6b	7a	IXb	22
VIII	5.11d	6b	7a	IXb	23
VIII+	5.12a	6b	7a+	IXc	24
IX−	5.12b	6c	7b	Xa	25
IX−	5.12c	6c	7b+	Xa	26
IX	5.12d	7a	7c	Xb	27
IX+	5.13a	7a	7c+	Xc	28
X−	5.13b	7b	8a	XIa	29
X−	5.13c	7b	8a+	XIa	30
X	5.13d	7b	8b	XIb	31
X+	5.14a	7b	8b+		32
XI−	5.14b		8c		33
XI−	5.14c		8c+		34
XI	5.14d		9a		

Index

About the Author

Ron Horton is originally from the Blue Ridge Mountains of Virginia and North Carolina, where he began climbing some fifteen years ago. He spent an abundance of time honing his rock skills at areas such as Seneca Rocks, Linville Gorge, and the New River Gorge, where he worked as a whitewater raft guide for several years. Ron moved to Olympia, Washington, in the mid-1990s, where he managed the Olympic Rock Gym. It was there that he developed a love for the Northwest, exploring the vast array of routes that Washington and Oregon have to offer, from the backcountry peaks of the Alpine Lakes to the knobby faces of Smith Rock.

Ron is a freelance writer and an English teacher at Clackamas High School, just outside of Portland, Oregon, where he currently resides. He has written two other books, both biographies on extreme athletes, entitled *Awesome Athletes* and *Extreme Athletes*.

Ron continues to pursue his love of the outdoors in the Northwest. He is an active climber, snowboarder, and fly-fisherman, and he

Ron Horton (Photo by Dana Griffin)

enjoys sharing these passions through his writing. He is currently in the masters program for writing at Portland State University, and he aspires to teach writing at the collegiate level.

About the Photographer

Lynn Willis (Photo by Courtney Loscheider)

A native of East Tennessee, Lynn Willis was introduced to climbing during the 1970s at summer camp in North Carolina. He discovered the joy of photography with his Brownie camera around the same time. In 1988 at the University of Tennessee he started climbing more seriously and spent most weekends on the steep sandstone of the Tennessee Wall in Chattanooga. Summers were spent traveling and climbing in the West or guiding rock climbing courses at Looking Glass Rock in North Carolina. With eighteen years of rock climbing and twelve years of ice climbing experience, Lynn has traveled all over the Southeast and made many trips to the Cascades, Tetons, Rockies, and the Sierras, as well as climbing trips to the Southwest desert, Mexico, and Canada. He has dozens of first ascent rock climbs and over 100 boulder problems to his credit. Lynn's portfolio includes images of adventure sports and mountain landscapes from the Appalachians to the Himalayas. He won first prize in the adventure category of the Appalachian Mountain Photography Competition and his photographs have been published in various outdoor catalogs and advertisements in *Rock & Ice, Climbing,* and *Blue Ridge Outdoors* magazines.

THE MOUNTAINEERS, founded in 1906, is a nonprofit outdoor activity and conservation club, whose mission is "to explore, study, preserve, and enjoy the natural beauty of the outdoors. . . . " Based in Seattle, Washington, the club is now the third-largest such organization in the United States, with seven branches throughout Washington State.

The Mountaineers sponsors both classes and year-round outdoor activities in the Pacific Northwest, which include hiking, mountain climbing, ski-touring, snowshoeing, bicycling, camping, kayaking, nature study, sailing, and adventure travel. The club's conservation division supports environmental causes through educational activities, sponsoring legislation, and presenting informational programs.

All club activities are led by skilled, experienced instructors, who are dedicated to promoting safe and responsible enjoyment and preservation of the outdoors.

If you would like to participate in these organized outdoor activities or the club's programs, consider a membership in The Mountaineers. For information and an application, write or call The Mountaineers, Club Headquarters, 300 Third Avenue West, Seattle, WA 98119; 206-284-6310. You can also visit the club's website at www.mountaineers.org or contact The Mountaineers via email at clubmail@mountaineers.org.

The Mountaineers Books, an active, nonprofit publishing program of the club, produces guidebooks, instructional texts, historical works, natural history guides, and works on environmental conservation. All books produced by The Mountaineers Books fulfill the club's mission.

Send or call for our catalog of more than 500 outdoor titles:

The Mountaineers Books
1001 SW Klickitat Way, Suite 201
Seattle, WA 98134
800-553-4453

mbooks@mountaineersbooks.org
www.mountaineersbooks.org

The Mountaineers Books is proud to be a corporate sponsor of The No Trace Center for Outdoor Ethics, whose mission is to promote and inspire responsible outdoor recreation through education, research, and partnerships. The Leave No Trace program is focused specifically on human-powered (nonmotorized) recreation.

Leave No Trace strives to educate visitors about the nature of their recreational impacts, as well as offer techniques to prevent and minimize such impacts. Leave No Trace is best understood as an educational and ethical program, not as a set of rules and regulations.

For more information, visit *www.LNT.org,* or call 800-332-4100.

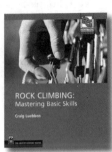
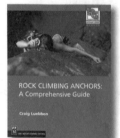